Introduc

Y **Bala** – meaning 'the outflow of the
on the shores of Llyn Tegid, the lar[
rounded by hills and mountains. It lies t
Snowdonia National Park on a natural fau.. ....
tant route into the heartland of Wales since prehistoric times, and later
became part of the Roman road system. At the heart of the district of
Penllyn, the town was created in 1310 by Roger de Mortimer to reinforce
English control of the district.

Despite its English origins, Y Bala is a strong Welsh-speaking
community that has produced renowned poets, politicians and preachers,
who have helped to shape cultural and religious life in Wales, and further
afield in Patagonia. In the 18th and early 19thC the town was renowned
for its knitted woollen gloves, stockings and caps. Today, it retains its
status as a small market town for the local farming community, and as a
centre of the Welsh language and culture.

The area is well known for its watersports, but it is also excellent
walking country. This new fully revised edition of my original book
explores its diverse scenery and history through 20 walks. It includes
new routes to hilltop forts and viewpoints now accessible on Open
Access land, as well as two linear walks (**19** & **20**) between Y Bala and
Llanuwchllyn, which when combined make a superb 14 mile upland
circuit of Llyn Tegid.

There are walks across pastureland, over open hills and moorland, by
rivers and lakes, through woods and forests. They offer extensive views
and visit many places of historical interest. The routes, which range from
1½ to 9 miles, follow public rights of way and permissive paths, or cross
Open Access land. A key feature is that most routes, as well as containing
shorter walk options, can easily be linked to provide longer and more
challenging day walks, if required.

Ensure that you are suitably prepared and equipped, especially on
the more exposed higher routes. Walking boots are required, along with
appropriate clothing to protect against the elements. Please remember
that the condition of paths can vary according to season and weather,
forest growth and clearance. If you encounter any problems with paths,
please refer these to Gwynedd Council (01341 422341).

Each walk has a detailed map and description, but be aware that
changes in detail can occur at any time. The location of each walk is
shown on the back cover and a summary of their key features is also
given. This includes an estimated walking time, but allow more time to
enjoy the scenery. Please observe the country code.

Enjoy your walking!

WALK I

Y BALA

DESCRIPTION A 4 mile orientation walk around Y Bala – a good introduction to the town, its history, notable buildings, and its scenic setting alongside Llyn Tegid, the rivers Tryweryn and Dee, surrounded by hills and mountains. Allow at least 3 hours for there is much to see. The route can easily be undertaken as two separate walks of 2½ and 1½ miles, and offers different starting points.

START Pont-y-Bala [SH 929362]

DIRECTIONS The stone bridge of Pont-y-Bala, which carries the A494 over the Afon Tryweryn, lies near the fire-station at the north eastern edge of town. A car park and toilets are nearby.

Walk across Pont y Bala to see the old stone arched gateway to Rhiwlas. Return across the bridge then cross the road to go through a small gate opposite to follow the signposted path along a wide grassy embankment parallel with the Afon Tryweryn. After passing a weir, cross a road, and continue on the green embanked path, close by a section of the river. After passing another weir, the path angles away from the Tryweryn to briefly join the infant river Dee – *which enters the lake at Llanuwchllyn as the Afon Dyfrdwy and is said to pass through 'without mingling the standing waters'* – before reaching the B4391. Cross the road and turn RIGHT to follow the pavement along the nearby side road – *offering superb views along Llyn Tegid.*

2 At a car park, take a tarmac path which runs near the shoreline of the lake, enjoying the view along the lake to the Arans. *Llyn Tegid, 4 miles long, nearly ¾ miles wide, and up to over 140 feet deep, is the largest freshwater lake in Wales. It contains the unique gwyniad – a whitefish member of the herring family imprisoned here after the Ice Age, when the lake was formed. It is rich in legends. One says that the lake is named after the mythical prince, Tegid Foel, whose town was one night engulfed by the huge lake in vengeance for his cruelty to his subjects. Another is that the valley was flooded after*

the keeper of St Gywair's holy well, forgot to replace the lid. Eventually, after passing the rear of the Leisure Centre/T.I.C. you reach the A494 by Loch Cafe. Turn RIGHT along the road towards the town centre. Just past the cinema, take the road on the left by the garage.

3 On the bend, take an enclosed path rising along a field edge to a road. Go up the road to pass the entrance to Penlan golf club, after which the road descends. On the bend take the signposted path into an access track on the right. Cross a stile and go along the field edge passing above the house, and on to cross a stile in the corner. Go along the next field edge, over another stile, and on past a ruin. Follow the old wall on your left into a field, and continue along its top edge across Craig y Fron, soon passing the remains of impressive caverns with stone pillar supports. *Stone was quarried here for the construction of Capel Tegid and other prominent buildings in Y Bala.* At their end descend to a stile and go down the field edge to another stile. Go past houses/bungalows to a road. Follow it RIGHT across the junction and down past the school into town. At cross-roads, follow the road RIGHT back to the garage passed earlier. Cross the main road.

4 Continue along the High Street past the Aran Factory shop – *a workhouse in the mid-19thC* – then the 17thC Ye Old Bull's Head and Barclay's Bank – *the former home of Thomas Charles (1755-1814) the great revivalist preacher. He came to the town in 1784, becoming one of the leaders of Welsh Methodism. He established the Sunday School system in Wales, wrote and published childrens' religious books, and produced cheap bibles which promoted literacy in North Wales. He also helped to found the British and Foreign Bible Society in 1804 after being inspired by Mary Jones. In 1860, 16 year old Mary, a poor weaver's daughter from Llanfihangel-y-Pennant, a hamlet lying behind the Cader Idris range, walked barefoot 25 miles over the mountains to Bala to buy a bible from him. Unfortunately he had sold them all, but he was so impressed with*

2

her efforts that he gave her his own copy.

5 Turn RIGHT down Tegid Street, past a traditional ironmongers shop and on to reach Capel Tegid. *The chapel, built in 1866 in memory of Thomas Charles, whose statue is nearby, was an important landmark of Nonconformist Wales.* Retrace your steps, then cross over to the 18thC White Lion Royal Hotel. *George Borrow, author of 'Wild Wales', stayed here twice during his walking tour in 1854. His lavish breakfast included eggs, mutton chops, salmon, trout and potted shrimps. He wrote 'I had never previously seen such a breakfast set before me'. The word 'Royal' was later added after Queen Victoria called at the hotel during her visit to Y Bala in 1889. Continue along the High Street – opposite is the 19thC Town Hall – to reach the statue of Thomas Edward Ellis (1859-99) – a Liberal M.P. and Chief Whip, who strove to achieve Welsh home rule, the disestablishment of the church in Wales, and better education. Go along Berwyn Street opposite. At its end is the former Independent College (1842-86), where* Michael D. Jones succeeded his father as Principal. He was a promoter of the venture in 1865, when 153 men, women and children sailed from Liverpool to establish a Welsh community in Patagonia, South America. Their descendants maintain strong ties with Wales, and many still speak Welsh.

6 Turn LEFT to reach Tomen y Bala *– believed to be a late 11thC Norman castle mound. It was later used for open-air preaching and by woollen knitters.* A key is available from the Council offices on the High Street. Continue to the junction, then turn RIGHT to finish at Neuadd y Cyfnod. *Originally a 17thC house, it was converted by Edmund Meyrick to a Free School in 1713. In the mid-19thC, it was rebuilt, with the main hall a replica of the one in Jesus College, Oxford, and it became a grammar school.*

3

WALK 2

PEN Y BWLCH GWYN & MOEL EMOEL

DESCRIPTION A 9 mile figure of eight walk (**A**) or easier 3 mile walk (**B**), through the varied countryside north of Y Bala, with extensive views. The main route rises in stages to explore a wild remote area of hills, now Open Access land, crossing Pen y Bwlch Gwyn (1646ft/502 m) by a choice of routes. It then either skirts or climbs the prominent hill of Moel Emoel (1801ft /549m) for superb views, passes an attractive upland lake, before crossing undulating country to finish with delightful riverside walking. Allow about 5½ hours. Walk B avoids the open hill section, which is for experienced walkers only and should be avoided in poor visibility.
START Near Pont Ty'n-y-ddol on the A4212 [SH 913384]
DIRECTIONS From Y Bala take the A4212 road towards Trawsfynydd. After about 1½ miles, it crosses the river (Pont Ty'n-y-ddol). 200 yards further is a small parking area on the right. Please do not block gateways. Alternatively, use a lay-by just before the river bridge.

I Cross a nearby stile and follow the access track up to Berth. Bear LEFT past outbuildings, then go through a waymarked gate on the right. Go half-LEFT, through a boundary gap and up the field edge to cross a stile. Continue up past a ruin to a lane. Follow it LEFT, then take a signposted path up a track on the right through a wood. Go up the field edge to a stile in the top left-hand corner. Keep ahead up the slope and on to a gate in a fence corner by Penmaen-mawr. (For **Walk B** turn right and resume text at point **6**)

2 Go through the gate and follow the fence on your left, past a waymarked gate and on up along the edge of an old reedy sunken track. Cross a stile in the fence just below a fence corner, and another stile above. Go up the right-hand side of a tree boundary and sunken track, later bending to cross a stile in a fence. Follow a path between walls up to a

forestry track. Follow the green track opposite to a gate. Go past a barn, then a small plantation, and on through a gate at another plantation corner – *with a view of Llyn Celyn*. Follow a green track ahead into open country – *with a view east to Moel Emoel* – to a gate. About 200 yards further take the right fork of the track. Shortly, the track bends up beneath another. Follow the fence on your left to a gate into Open Access land. Continue down to another gate, past a ruin, and on above an old stone boundary. After a gate at its corner keep ahead, soon on a rising path beneath a fence, which you follow to a stile. Continue ahead on a faint green track, which then rises to a gate.

3 Here you have a choice: For higher **route A**, climb the high ground ahead to enjoy extensive views, then go N.E. across the wide undulating tussocky top of Pen y Bwlch Gwyn to cross a fence. Follow it RIGHT down to its corner at point 4. For **route B**, after 30 yards, angle down to join a clear path below, which contours across the upper slopes of Pen y Bwlch Gwyn. After 200 yards take the left fork gently descending then continuing across the hillside. When it fades, maintain height and direction, before briefly descending then continuing to a fence corner. Follow the fence to cross it just before a sheepfold. Go half-RIGHT up the slope ahead to pass small rock outcrops and on across the moorland towards Moel Emoel, soon descending to a fence corner.

4 Follow a clear path beside the fence. After a gate, the path continues to a prominent viewpoint of Llyn Tegid, then briefly descends. Just beyond a second area of small rock outcrops, follow a fainter path bending LEFT through reeds towards Moel Emoel. After 75 yards you have another choice. For **route A**, head up to a large boulder and follow a clear path, later disappearing, to climb up the northern slopes of Moel Emoel to its summit cairn for panoramic views. Follow a good path down its southern slopes. As it begins to level out, at a crosspath about 250 yards before the forest, turn RIGHT and follow the clear path down the hillside to a stile/gate. (For **route B** follow

4

a green track contouring around the lower western slopes, before passing through a short boggy section. When the path splits near Llyn Maen Bras, take the LEFT fork to a stile/gate.)

5 Go down a green track to a gate. Cross the track, and go on down through a gate further ahead. Follow a waymarked path down to a stile and on through a small wood, then along the edge of two fields. Go through a gate in the corner and bear half-RIGHT to clip the end of a tree boundary. Continue past a telegraph pole, then a waymark post down to cross a stream, then bear RIGHT up to cross a stile. Follow the field edge round to a stile in the corner. Continue beside a stream, cross another stile and the stream ahead. Go up a track, then bear RIGHT past a barn and on between a ruin and Penmaen-canol cottage, then bear LEFT through a gate. Go across the field, past gates on your left (the second giving access to an alternative link route as shown) to follow the fence up to a stile. Go through a small wood and on across open ground to eventually pass behind Penmaen-mawr to a familiar gate.

6 Go along its access track. On the bend go up the slope ahead and across the middle of a field to a ladder-stile. Head down towards a farm. Go through a gate by a barn, then follow the farm's access track to a lane. Follow it LEFT for ¼ mile then take a signposted path on the right. Go half-LEFT, soon descending towards a farm to go through a gate below. Follow a green track, then farm access track to the road. Turn RIGHT, then shortly LEFT on a signposted path along a track. Follow it down to the Afon Tryweryn, then go through the large field to cross a stile at the far end. Follow a delightful way-marked stiled riverside path through a wood and fields, and on with a path to rejoin Berth's access drive.

5

WALK 3
BEYOND LLANFOR

DESCRIPTION A 5½ mile walk (**A**) through the undulating countryside just to the north-east of Y Bala. The route takes you to the attractive ancient community of Llanfor, with its Victorian church and interesting churchyard, before meandering on paths, forestry tracks and quiet lanes through part of the Rhiwlas estate, passing old farms and offering good views. Allow about 3¼ hours. The route can easily be shortened to a 4½ mile walk (**B**) from Llanfor or a short 1½ mile walk (**C**) between Y Bala and Llanfor.
START Pont-y-Bala [SH 929362] or alternatively Llanfor [SH 938367]
DIRECTIONS The stone bridge of Pont-y-Bala, which carries the A494 over the Afon Tryweryn, lies near the fire-station at the eastern edge of Y Bala town. A car park and toilets are nearby. Llanfor lies within a mile of Y Bala just off the A494.

1 From the north side of the bridge walk along the A494 – *passing the old arched gateway leading to Rhiwlas Hall.* Follow the pavement, part-screened by hedge/trees, past a stile opposite a house, to cross another stile further along. Go half-RIGHT across a large field to reach the road at Llanfor. Turn RIGHT and walk through the village to the church. *Built in 1875, it stands on the site of the oldest church in Merionydd that once served this large parish. Among the intricately carved headstones is the grave of a man who survived 27 battles, including Waterloo. The unusual large stone building at the top of the churchyard has a tale to tell. The inscription above the doorway reads: 'As to my latter end I go to seek my Jubilee, I bless the good horse Bendigo, who built this tomb for me' This mausoleum of Richard John Lloyd Price of Rhiwlas Hall – a famous sportsman, author and founder of a shortlived Welsh Whiskey Distillery at Fron Goch – was paid for by a wager on the horse Bendigo that won the Kempton Park Jubilee in the year he died-1887.*

2 Leave the church by the side gate. (For **Walk C** go back along the road out of the village to take the signposted path on the left at point **5**.) For the main route, turn RIGHT on a signposted path along a green track that passes behind the mausoleum. At its end, go through a small wooden gate, then go up the field to join a farm track. *In an adjoining field is the remains of an earthwork castle of late 11thC Norman origin or late Welsh revival.* Go up the track and just past a shale rock-face, as the track bends half-right, follow a path ahead for a few yards. At the fence corner, go across open ground towards a transmitter mast on the hill ahead, to pass through an old embanked field boundary, just to the right of a telegraph pole. Keep ahead, soon along the right-hand bank of a stream. Just past a solitary tree leave the stream to go through a waymarked gate in the fence corner ahead. After crossing the stream, continue between small trees then follow a clear path angling up across the bracken-covered slope, and on alongside the perimeter fence of a wood to cross a stile. Continue up alongside the wood/field boundary – *with good views across the Dee valley.*

3 Just before a stile in the top field corner, turn RIGHT to cross another stile on the left by a gate. Follow the fence on your left through two fields, then pass through an old farm. Follow its access track to ford a stream and on to reach a lane. Turn LEFT up the lane, then shortly turn RIGHT along a wide forestry road. When it splits after ¼ mile continue on the track ahead (the other leads to Creigiau-isaf) for a further ½ mile through the partly felled forest. After passing telegraph pole no. 14 and a path on the left, and just before the track bends right, you meet a waymarked path angling in from the secluded house of Creigau-uchaf on your right. Here take a short waymarked path on the left past telegraph poles to cross a stile into a field. Go towards buildings ahead, later following an old green track to the old farm. Bear half-LEFT past the right-hand side of the building on the left, over a stream, then go past the hinged side of a gate in the fence corner to follow the fence on your right down the field edge and through the facing gate in the corner – *with views of the Berwyns, Llyn Tegid and the Arans.* Turn RIGHT along the field edge, then bend LEFT down the edge of mixed woodland to a stile in the field corner. Cross a track and follow a waymarked path through a small area of birch, very soon bearing RIGHT to cross a stile.

4 Continue ahead with the old hedge boundary on your right, past a waymarked tree stump to go between two large stones in the old boundary ahead. Keep ahead for about 30 yards then bear LEFT back along an old green track to cross a stream/wettish area. Keep ahead with the old boundary on the left for a few yards, then bear RIGHT to follow a path below a small bracken-covered rocky knoll and across open ground – *with a view of Llyn Tegid.* Pass just to the left *to walk 2* of a telegraph pole and below a pylon, then before the gateway just ahead, work your way down below the boundary to a nearby ruined farm. Continue along its old access track, soon passing a plantation. After going through a gate at its corner, leave the track and head half-LEFT down the field, through a gate in the corner, and on down the next field edge to cross a stile onto a minor country road. Follow it LEFT to join another road by a wood. Continue along the road, past a house and an alternative link path. A few hundred yards after passing an Electric sub-station, take a signposted path on the right.

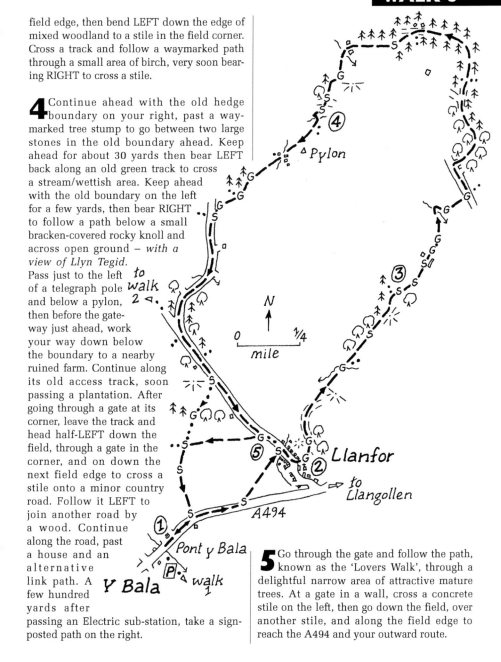

5 Go through the gate and follow the path, known as the 'Lovers Walk', through a delightful narrow area of attractive mature trees. At a gate in a wall, cross a concrete stile on the left, then go down the field, over another stile, and along the field edge to reach the A494 and your outward route.

WALK 4
LLYN CAER-EUNI

DESCRIPTION A 5⅓ mile walk (**A**), with good views, through a little known area of attractive low upland pasture and valleys, passing near an ancient standing stone, and the site of a cock pit, to visit a delightful hidden lake. Allow about 3 hours. The route can easily be shortened to a 4 mile walk (**B**).

START Sarnau [SH 972393]

DIRECTIONS Leave Y Bala on the A494 towards Corwen, and after about 4 miles, turn left into the hamlet of Sarnau. Park tidily on the roadside.

*S**arnau** was once an important crossing point of two ancient routes. Before a turnpike road (now the A494) was built the main valley road went through the village. It had an inn and a smithy. The first stone house on the left (note the arch in the gable end) has an interesting history. It was built as a church, but before it was consecrated, it was used as a hospital after smallpox broke out in the area. It later became a church school. Opposite Sarnau is Coers y Sarnau nature reserve, a patchwork of wetland habitat and woodland owned by the North Wales Wildlife Trust.*

I Walk up the road, then take the side road on the left between cottages. Go up the road for about 100 yards, then take a signposted path along a track on the left – *with good views west to the Arans.* Follow it up to Ty Hen. Just before the house, cross a stile on the left and follow the boundary on your right. Go over a cross-track and keep ahead up the edge of a field to follow a tree boundary round to cross a stile. Turn RIGHT to enter another field and walk along its edge. In the corner follow the signposted diverted path alongside the fence passing behind a cottage to cross a stile onto its access track. Follow it to a road. *Prominent among the reedy pasture is a standing stone, which once marked the line of an old road from Llangwm to Llandderfel. Ahead at the road is Coed y Bedo, a small old Welsh Manor house, once the home of Bedo Aeddren, a 15thC poet.* Turn LEFT (or right for **Walk B**) and follow the road down the valley, then take the first side road on the right. Follow the tree-lined road up the attractive wooded side valley. After a gate, the road enters a more open section of the valley.

2 Just after a waymarked path on the left, go through a waymarked gate on the right. Go up the field to cross a stock gate in the top left-hand corner. Cross a green track and go up the slope ahead, passing between clumps of trees. The land soon levels out above a small wooded side valley. Continue ahead to cross a ladder-stile into an area of attractive upland pasture. Keep ahead, then go up through bracken to cross a stone stile, then continue down a reedy green track and along a small valley to go through a gate into Open Access land. Here you can simply follow the track to its bend and nearby stile. A more rewarding alternative is to bear RIGHT to pass the pylon, and climb onto the nearby ridge top for extensive all-round views, then head NE over subsidiary tops to descend to the bend of the track. *Alongside the track is a small circular mound – the remains of a cock pit. Cock-fighting was once popular in the area.* Cross the stile ahead and keep alongside the wall to descend to a road. Follow it LEFT, soon descending into the attractive wooded valley of Cwm Main – *once occupied by Quakers.*

3 On the bend at the bottom of the hill, turn RIGHT on the signposted path, then take the right fork of the lane past the end of 18thC Capel Rhydywernen – *still serving the local community.* Descend between the cottage and an outbuilding to follow an enclosed path down to cross a footbridge over a stream. Turn LEFT and follow the stream along the edge of a long field to cross a stile at its end. Follow the path past conifers and on to cross a stile. Continue through the edge of a plantation to enter a field. Go ahead for about 200 yards, then go half-RIGHT up to a waymark post beneath a wood. Follow a path rising across the wooded slope to cross a stile. Turn LEFT along a green track,

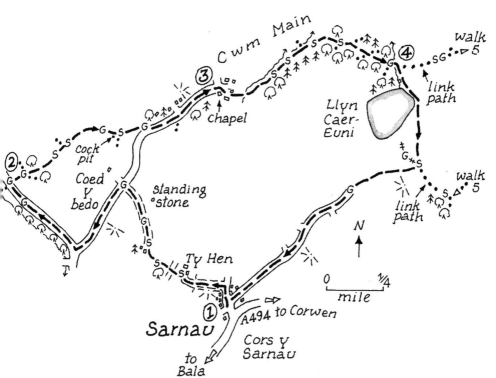

then after about 20 yards, take a waymarked path on the right, angling up through conifers to cross a stony track. Continue on the waymarked path up a green track angling through deciduous trees. At the end of the wood, when the track swings sharp right, go through the gate ahead and across a stream. Keep ahead briefly, then bend RIGHT up and across a wettish area to reach an old sheepfold. *Almost unexpectedly, just ahead lie the tranquil waters of Llyn Caer-Euni. It is said that here late at night you may see a horned shepherd collecting his sheep – reputed to be Cernunnos the Celtic God of Nature and the Underworld.*

4 Follow the path ahead to the lake – where large rocks make a scenic stopping place – and along the end of the lake, boggy in places. At its corner, angle half-RIGHT away from the lake with an intermittent path over rough wet ground to pass the left-hand side of a rock covered slope ahead. Continue in the same direction, soon rising

on a clear path through bracken, then up a reedy slope. Go past a gate to your right, levelling out to cross a stile by another gate near the fence corner on the open ridge – *with good views of the Berwyns, the Arans, Cader Idris, and Arenig Fawr.* Keep ahead to follow a steadily improving green track west to a gate and on with a lane – *offering good views of Llyn Tegid –* back down to the start.

9

WALK 5

CAER EUNI

DESCRIPTION A meandering 5½ mile walk (**A**), with extensive views, exploring an attractive upland area, now designated Open Access land, once occupied by early man. It visits two important early historical sites – an impressive Iron-Age hillfort (1197 feet/365 metres high) and Bronze Age ceremonial/burial circles. The route includes a shorter 3 mile walk (**B**) and can easily be extended to include Llyn Caer-Euni. Allow about 3½ hours.

START Bethel [SH 988398]

DIRECTIONS Leave Y Bala on the A494 towards Corwen, and after nearly 5 miles, upon reaching the hamlet of Bethel, turn left on a minor road opposite the B4402 (Llandderfel). A small parking space is immediately on the left.

B ethel, so named after a chapel was built here in the early 19thC, was an important stopping place for drovers. They stayed at The Boot – an inn up to the 1930s – and their cattle were kept in a field opposite. There was a smithy, and at one time a school. The minor road is on the line of the Roman road running east from Caergai to Chester.

I Walk along the road past the former chapel, and on past Blaen Cwm. About 250 yards beyond, take a signposted path on the left, heading back through the trees above the road. It soon does a sharp u-turn and rises steadily across the slope to leave the wood by a stile. Continue ahead following the boundary on your right. At the field corner, bear LEFT to cross a ladder-stile, and keep ahead to go along an embankment to cross another stile. Turn RIGHT through a wet area and follow the fence to join a track. Follow it for about 150 yards, then just before a gate across it, turn LEFT. Now follow a path across reedy ground, parallel with the boundary, later running closer to the fence to go through a facing gateway in the far fence corner. Continue up to the hill-fort and its summit cairn for all-round views, including Llantisilio Mountain, Clwydian Hills, Arenig, Cader Idris, the Arans, and the Berwyns. *Caer Euni hillfort dates from the*

1st millennium. It is a long narrow fort that utilises the natural defence of a steep slope on its south-east side, with ramparts and a ditch on its north-west side, and an entrance at the north-east. The original fort was later enlarged and strengthened to the south-west. Return to the gateway, then head half-RIGHT across tussocky ground to cross a stile by a gate in the fence on your right. (For **Walk B**, just ahead bear left to follow the path up to the stone circles.)

2 Turn RIGHT and descend to pass beneath nearby bracken, then follow a path down to a stile. Continue along the field edge to another stile and on to reach a lane. Go up the lane. At a signposted cross-path, turn LEFT down the access track to Tyn-yr-Erw and cross a stile just to the left of the cottage. Turn LEFT along the field edge, through a gap in the corner, then go half-RIGHT on the waymarked path to descend through trees, over a stream, and on over a ladder-stile. Go down the field to cross a stile in the bottom right-hand corner by a wood. Turn LEFT and follow the path, guided by a series of yellow-topped poles, through the wood to reach a stony track.

3 Go through the gate opposite, then turn LEFT up the field edge to pass through a gap. *Ahead lies the attractive wooded valley of Cwm Main, once occupied by Quakers.* Continue along the next field edge and after about 150 yards, cross a stile in the fence. Keep ahead for 40 yards to reach a green track. Follow it RIGHT, past a game-bird rearing area, then follow the waymarked path to a stile and on along the bottom edge of attractive woodland. After a gateway, the path crosses open bracken-covered slopes, passes through a gate, then continues along a green track. About 50 yards after an old cattle-grid, and just before the ruin of Tyddyn Tyfod – *once occupied by Edward ap Rhys, who went with the first group of Welsh Quakers to Pennsylvania in 1682* – turn LEFT up past a wall to follow a path rising beside an old tree boundary to a stile. Continue up the path across the bracken-covered slope.

10

4 At the top go through a gateway. Turn LEFT and continue near the moorland edge. After crossing a stream at the top of a gully, follow a path towards a large tree ahead. Now go up the open slope to the highest point for all-round views (or continue past the tree and beneath the craggy slopes) then descend south. At the bottom of the slope turn LEFT. After a stile in the fence, keep ahead, then just before a boundary corner, turn RIGHT on a clear path. When it splits after a few yards, take the left fork past a boundary corner, then the right fork across moorland to reach a clear cross path. Follow it RIGHT up to the remains of Cefn Caer-Euni bronze age stone circles at a good viewpoint. *Dating from the late 3rd millennium BC., the large kerb circle and a smaller ring cairn were used for ceremonial and burial purposes. The large circle was said to have been used as a cockpit in the 18thC when cockfighting was popular in the area. There is evidence of domestic settlement on this exposed ridge pre-dating the circles.*

yards to a stile below, go onto a small ridge ahead, then descend from an upland shelf to join a fence below trees, which you follow right to a stile.) Follow the green track to cross a stile by a gate. Turn LEFT and follow the fence down – *with a view of Llyn Tegid* – to a stile at the wood corner. Go down the slope below the fence, and after about 120 yards, do a sharp u-turn down the old reedy track to a stile. Now follow the left-hand edge of the old track and go past the side of a house to the road by the start.

5 Continue along the path to a gate, and across the broad moorland ridge to a stile between two gates. From the left-hand gate go along an old green track – *soon with a view of Llyn Caer-Euni nestling below.* (After 200 yards, another descent option is to go half-left over a bracken-covered ridge after 200

Map labels: Tyn-yr-Erw · Cwm Main · ③ · Tyddyn Tyfod · N · fort · walk 4 · ② · ④ · ⑤ circles · Llyn Caer-Euni · walk 4 · Blaen Cwm · ① · Bethel · P · to Y Bala · A4402 · A4494 · to Llanderfel · 0 · ¼ · mile

Llyn Caer-Euni

WALK 6

MYNYDD MYNYLLOD

DESCRIPTION This meandering 7½ mile figure of eight walk (**A**) rises from the Upper Dee valley through its part wooded lower slopes to explore delightful hidden upland pasture, with its rocky outcrops, scattered trees, old stone walls and former farms, and moorland north east of Llandderfel. It rises in easy stages to just over 1200 feet and offers superb views. Allow about 4 hours. It can easily be shortened to a 4½ mile walk (**B**), or varied using a link road.

START Llandderfel [SH 982371]

DIRECTIONS See **Walk 7** for directions and information on Llanderfel.

I Follow the road over the stream and past the toilets. When it splits, keep on the RIGHT fork, passing an old chapel. *It contained an 1868 commemorative stone to John Jones, Ellis Roberts and Mary Jones (mother of Michael D. Jones – the founder of the Patagonia community) who were turned out of their homes after the 1859 Election by their Tory landlords for voting for a Liberal MP. Like others, they had become empowered from learning to read through religion and posed a threat to the landed gentry. The stone is now in the Neuadd Derfel.* Continue along this quiet country road – *enjoying good views of the river Dee.*

2 After ¾ mile, take a signposted path through a gate on the left, opposite a large roadside stone house and outbuildings. Go up the field to cross a stile above a stream into a wood. Now follow a path along the wood edge, soon joining a green track rising half-LEFT. After about 75 yards head up through the trees to the top wood boundary fence. Follow it past a yellow topped post and over a stile just beyond. When the fence bends up left, follow a faint path ahead through the trees for 75 yards, rising to another post. Angle slightly LEFT to pass a further post and on up to go through a small gate. Follow the fence up the field. At the fence corner turn RIGHT. Follow the

waymarked path down to a facing gate, and on alongside the fence past a nearby house, down to the bottom field corner. Turn LEFT. Go past the left-hand side of a small pool and through a wet area to cross a stile ahead by the stream. Go through the small gate, up the green track and through a large gate. Follow the fence on your right round past another gate to go through a gate in the top field corner. Turn LEFT along the green track, soon rising past a small wood, then passing a track on the left, to eventually reach Cae-pant. Follow its access lane to a road. Turn RIGHT. The road soon rises steadily.

3 Just past the entrance to Ty'n-y-fron, take a signposted bridleway on the left. After a gate, it goes along a green track, then bends up the field edge to Cae lago, before continuing RIGHT alongside a fence. After passing a small stone sheepfold, go up the gorse-covered slope ahead and over a faint green track. Keep ahead, soon descending and passing a reedy area to go through a gate. Continue up a green track and on across the upland pasture to reach a gate in the boundary corner ahead – *with extensive views towards Y Bala, the Arans, Cader Idris and Arenig Fawr.* (For **Walk B**, turn left and resume text at point **6**.)

4 Go through the gate. Ignore the descending track. Instead follow another faint green track ahead, then go past a reedy area and up to go through a gate. Keep ahead, then turn RIGHT through a gate in the field corner and on up a green track. After another gate, turn LEFT off the track and follow the wall down to cross a stile just beyond its end. Go ahead to skirt the left-hand side of a large marshy area. Just beyond a small lake cross a stile and stream on the right into Open Access land. Bear LEFT up a faint green track, soon bending RIGHT and rising alongside a fence. At the fence corner, turn LEFT, continuing up by the fence. At the next fence corner, where the path levels out, go half-RIGHT across a reedy area for 25 yards. (Here, a path can be followed up and across the part heather-covered broad ridge – *for all-round views* – soon descending, then bearing left just before a wall corner and descending to the stile at point 5.) For the main route turn LEFT and follow a path along the edge of the large marshy area – *with views of Llantisilio Mountain and the Clwydian Hills.* About 100 yards before a gate ahead, swing RIGHT through bracken to cross a stile in the fence ahead by an old gate.

5 Follow the wall across the open moorland of Mynydd Mynyllod, then a path alongside an old wall. At its end, the path descends then crosses a wettish area. About 75 yards before a sheepfold, go through a gate in

Mynydd Mynyllod

sheepfold

ruin

sheepfold

Cae-Iago

Cae-Pant

N

0   ¼   mile

walk 7

Llandderfel

River Dee

fence. When it bends right, keep ahead to go through a waymarked wall gap, then follow a green track to go through an old gateway in the wall ahead. After it fades, keep ahead across upland pasture to go through a gap in an old low wall. Now go slightly LEFT, soon descending to rejoin your outward path by a stile. Retrace your steps to go through the gate at point **4**.

6 Continue ahead, keeping alongside the boundary on your right, to steadily descend the hillside to eventually cross a stile above a former farm. Pass between buildings and follow its access track down to a road. Follow it LEFT, past a signposted path, then go through a recessed gate on your left, opposite two on your right. Descend the path, then bend RIGHT down to go through a gate. Go past the house and on along its access track. Just beyond a second house, turn LEFT through iron gates, bear RIGHT through a gate ahead and go along the left-hand side of a paddock to cross a stile into a wood. Turn RIGHT and go through the wood edge above the stream and on along the edge of three fields to the road. Turn RIGHT back to the start.

the fence on your right. Continue alongside an old boundary, through another gate, and on down the path – *with views towards Llyn Tegid.* Near the bottom go half-LEFT to follow a fence to go through a gate in it. Follow the boundary on your left, soon on a path descending through gorse to join a green track, then go along an access track from a nearby cottage. Just before a gate and lane, cross a stile up on the right. Go over a footbridge, then angle LEFT to a waymarked fence corner. Follow the boundary on your right up the slope and through a wall gap near a ruin. Follow the fence to cross a stile in the gorse-covered corner. Keep with the

LLYN MAES Y CLAWDD & EARL'S WOOD

DESCRIPTION A delightful 4¼ mile walk in the beautiful Upper Dee valley featuring two attractive lakes, woodland, and extensive views. Part of the route is known locally as the Queen's Walk, for its association with Queen Victoria's visit to the area in 1889. Allow about 2½ hours.

START Llandderfel [SH 982371]

DIRECTIONS Leave Y Bala on the A494 towards Llangollen, then turn right on the B4401. At a war memorial, turn left into the peaceful village of Llanderfel. Take the first road right, to park alongside a stream opposite the National School dating from 1828. Toilets are nearby.

*L*landderfel *takes its name from St Derfel Gadarn – Derfel the Mighty – a famous 6thC warrior-saint. The early Christian saints often used the old pagan religion to promote Christianity. St Derfel adopted the same powers as Cernunnos, the god of Nature and the Underworld, who had stag antlers on his head. The church was dedicated to him and many pilgrims came to the village in the Middle Ages to pray to his large wooden image, often bringing animals to be cured and blessed. The tradition that the image would set forests on fire was strangely fulfilled, when in 1538, on the orders of Thomas Cromwell, who wanted to root out superstitious practices, it was removed and publicly burned at Smithfield, London, along with Friar Forest of Greenwich, who was accused of high treason. His wooden stag, without its antlers, which had encouraged pagans to believe that Cernnunos was willing to accept the new religion, is all that remains from the famous shrine and now stands in the church porch. However, it continued to play an important role in village life. Each Easter Tuesday, the 'horse' would be brought out and carried in procession to a hill near St Derfel's Well. It would then be converted into a ride for local children.*

The present church dates from the 15thC. In 1758, the fine oak roof was destroyed by fire. Remnants of it were used in Plas Newydd, the house occupied by the famous 'Ladies of Llangollen'.

Llandderfel is well known for its literary figures. The poet Huw Cae Llwyd visited Rome in 1475 and wrote a famous poem about the relics he saw there, including one which appears very much like the Turin Shroud. Edward Jones, known as 'Barad y Brenin' – the King's Poet – was harpist to the Prince of Wales in 1790. He collected and published many volumes of Welsh music. Other famous sons are R. J. Berwyn, a radical, who wrote hymns and Welsh periodicals, the 19thC poet Dewi Hafhest, and the local historian Evan Roberts. A slate quarry and the nearby Pale estate provided employment for local people.

I Return to the main road in the village. Turn RIGHT past the church and follow the road out of the village, then turn LEFT on a road signposted to Cefn-ddwysarn. It rises steadily, passing Ty-newydd. After ½ mile, when the road bends sharp right, continue ahead along the access track leading to Ty'n-y-bwlch. *After the effort of an early climb, you are rewarded with extensive views, including the Berwyns to the south and the Arans to the west. Follow the track past Llyn Maes y Clawdd – a small upland lake, which provides fishing and bird-watching facilities specifically for people with disabilities, following an initiative by the landowners in partnership with statutory and voluntary bodies and the local community. R. Williams Parry, when head of Sarnau school in 1913, regularly used to walk past Llyn Maes y Clawdd to visit his sister, who was the minister's wife in Llanderfel. He wrote a poem about his journey, telling of hearing owls hooting in the nearby woods.* After a gate continue along the track passing below the house and gently descending to go through the right of two facing gates. Continue ahead along the edge of the long field – *with views of distant Llyn Tegid* – later descending to cross a stile in its corner. Now follow a stiled path down and along the edge of Coed Bryn

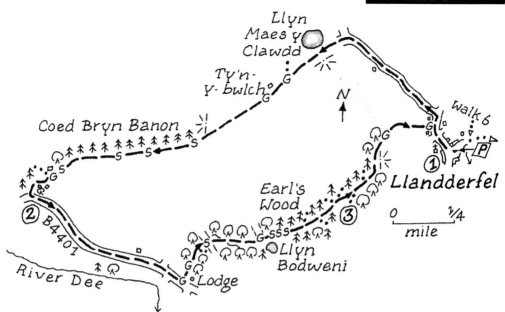

Banon to reach an old farm. Pass between farm buildings and continue down its stony access track to the B4401.

2 Cross the road, turn LEFT and follow the attractive valley road for about ¾ mile. *In the 1890s, engineers from London came to survey the possibility of making a dam by Bodweni, where the Dee valley is narrow. The resulting lake would have drowned Y Bala. According to the plan, Y Bala would have been rebuilt between Cefn-ddwysarn and Llanderfel!* After a right-hand bend – *with a good view of the river Dee* – take a signposted path through a gate on the left, just before Bodweni Lodge to begin the Queen's Walk. Go ahead across the field to pass through a gate by a small wood. Go up the path for about 50 yards to a waymarked fence corner, then head almost half-LEFT across open ground to a waymark post by mature woodland. Continue ahead soon joining a faint green track which bends up to a stile onto a broad track. The waymarked path now turns LEFT down a stony track, then after a few yards turns RIGHT up a green track alongside a stream through an attractive area of woodland. The track crosses the stream and continues to rise, soon passing conifers to pass

through a gate by attractive Llyn Bodweni. Continue straight ahead over a track past the end of the lake to cross a stile at the wood corner. Go along the wood edge, over another stile and on up to cross a further stile in the corner. Now follow a clear waymarked path through Earl's Wood, shortly descending then bearing half-left. Soon the path rises gently to pass a waymark post on the right.

3 Just beyond are two tracks. Take the right one angling down through the trees and along the wood edge to pass a prominent viewpoint. *Below lies Llandderfel nestling in the part-wooded Dee valley, with the Berwyns beyond. The large house across the valley to your right is Pale Hall, built in 1868 for Henry Robertson, the famous railway engineer, responsible for the impressive Chirk viaduct across the Dee. In 1889, Queen Victoria, with 76 servants, arrived by train at a nearby station for a short stay at Pale. The princes were taken to Ruabon to see a coal mine and travelled on coal trucks lined with velvet!* Leave the wood by an old gate and follow the green track down the hillside to reach the road at Llandderfel. Turn RIGHT back to the start.

WALK 8
BWLCH-Y-FENNI & GARTH GOCH

DESCRIPTION A 6¾ mile walk (**A**) exploring an area of upland grassland and forest southeast of Y Bala, with excellent views. The main route rises in stages to the ancient high pass of Bwlch-y-Fenni (1385 feet/422 metres), and later provides views of the old manor house of Plas Rhiwaedog, before visiting Garth Goch, the site of the first recorded sheep dog trial. Allow about 4 hours. The route includes a shorter 5 mile walk (**B**).

START River bridge, Rhos-y-gwaliau [SH 944346] or the riverside car park, Cwm Hirnant [SH 955337].

DIRECTIONS Take the B4391 south from Y Bala, then turn right on a road signposted to Rhos-y-gwaliau. Go through Rhos-y-gwaliau to find limited informal off-road parking on the no through road by the bridge/river. Alternatively, continue along the road for about 1 mile to a riverside car park just past Tyn-y-cwm. (From here, take a nearby signposted path rising through the trees, continuing up alongside the fence to point **2**).

I Cross the bridge over the river, and just past a side road, take a signposted path on the left, which rises across the tree-covered slope above the road. Soon take the left fork up across the higher slope to cross a stile at the top of the wood. Go ahead for a few yards, then head half-RIGHT between rock outcrops and across the part tree-covered slope to cross a ladder-stile at a forest corner. Go up alongside the forest boundary fence, over a stile, and on alongside the fence. At its corner, continue ahead across reedy ground to cross a ladder-stile. Keep ahead, soon following a track up to go through a gate. Bear RIGHT alongside the fence for about 100 yards.

2 At a waymark post in the fence, briefly head half-LEFT, then go up through a gap in the slope, then bear RIGHT, soon alongside a fence rising towards a forest. At a waymarked post in the fence, about 150 yards below the field corner, go half-RIGHT up the slope to cross a stile in the top fence – *with good views looking back over Y Bala to Arenig* – to a path just beyond. (For **Walk B**, turn left and follow the path along the forest edge, soon descending past a waymark post. Now go half-right up a forestry road (a permissive route with the kind permission of the landowners). It levels out to contour around the hillside, then begins to descend, soon swinging sharp left. Follow it down to a farm to rejoin the main route at point **5**.)

3 Turn RIGHT and follow the gently rising path across the gorse/heather/conifer covered slope, soon joining a forestry track. Follow it RIGHT, later rising steadily to cross a forestry road. Continue up the green track ahead, and on through the forest to eventually cross another forestry road. Take a short path opposite to leave the forest via a stile. Go down the field and through a gate at the entrance to Maes-hir – a mid-19thC estate farm. Turn LEFT to pass between the outbuilding with a clock tower weather vane and the house. Follow its gated access lane up what was once an important route between the Hirnant and the Dee valleys to reach the high pass of Bwlch-y-Fenni. Go past two signposted paths on the right, then go half-LEFT up a green track. Soon, go through a waymarked gateway and follow the fence on your right, through another gate, and on past a forest to cross a stile at its corner.

4 Continue ahead alongside the fence – *enjoying views of the Upper Dee Valley.* At the waymarked fence corner/stile, continue along the right-hand edge of a bending heather-banked old sunken green path. After a waymark post the now open path continues down and across the bracken-covered eastern slopes of craggy Craigiau y bwlch, loosely parallel with the fence to your right. After crossing a stile in an old gateway, continue ahead, passing between rock outcrops, then descending to pass a waymark post and cross a stile at the far side of a reedy area. Go half-LEFT across the reedy field and down to cross a step stile in the bottom corner – *with views over Y Bala to the Arenigs.* Follow a

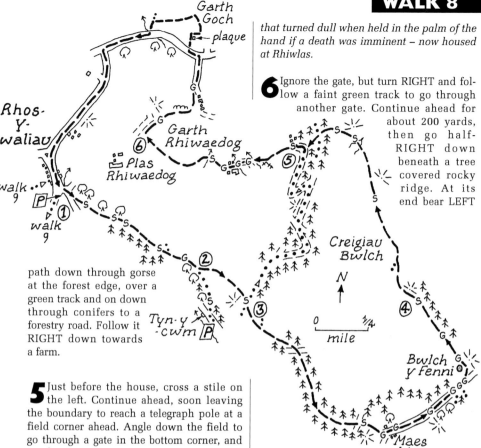

that turned dull when held in the palm of the hand if a death was imminent – now housed at Rhiwlas.

6 Ignore the gate, but turn RIGHT and follow a faint green track to go through another gate. Continue ahead for about 200 yards, then go half-RIGHT down beneath a tree covered rocky ridge. At its end bear LEFT

path down through gorse at the forest edge, over a green track and on down through conifers to a forestry road. Follow it RIGHT down towards a farm.

5 Just before the house, cross a stile on the left. Continue ahead, soon leaving the boundary to reach a telegraph pole at a field corner ahead. Angle down the field to go through a gate in the bottom corner, and on along a track to a farm. Go ahead past the house and outbuildings to go through a gate on the right by a finger post. Go along the field edge to cross a stile in the corner. Cross a stream and walk ahead for 100 yards, then bear half-LEFT to skirt round the slopes of Garth Rhiwaedog, soon alongside a fence on your left to eventually reach a gate by an access track leading to Plas Rhiwaedog. *It was the home of Rhivid Flaidd, Lord of Penllyn circa 1160 and later that of the Llwyd family, who rebuilt the hall in the 17thC. It was renowned for its defensive qualities and hospitality to visiting poets, scholars and clergy. In the 18thC, William Jones – a keen nonconformist – accommodated people attending preaching festivals on Y Bala Green each summer. It was said to contain treasures in secret rooms, including a rare relic of Owain Gwynedd – a crystal*

to pass above a farm and on through a gate in the corner. Follow its access lane down to a road. Cross the road and turn LEFT. Shortly, at a road sign take a path on the right to a plaque set in a large boulder on the lower slopes of Garth Goch, now an Open Access area. *It records the first sheep dog trial held on 9th October 1873.* Follow a path from behind the boulder up to the grass summit of Garth Goch, then another heading north to several large boulders. Immediately after the largest boulder, bear LEFT to follow a clear path down the slope and across the fine grasses to a waymark post, where a path leads LEFT to the road. Turn RIGHT across the bridge over an impressive gorge. Continue up the road, then take a minor road on the left and follow it into Rhos-y-gwaliau.

WALK 9
AROUND CWM HIRNANT & CWM CYMERIG

DESCRIPTION A 5½ mile walk (**A**) that explores the attractive valleys and upland pasture south of Rhos-y-gwaliau, with good views. The route crosses the lower open slopes of Cwm Hirnant, returns to the valley then climbs part tree-covered slopes and crosses upland pasture. After a short rough section of forest it descends to Cwm Cymerig and continues along the wide ridge of Mynydd Cefn-ddwy-Graig, now a designated Open Access area. Allow about 3½ hours. The route includes two easier shorter walks – a 2½ mile walk (**B**) up Cwm Cymerig and along Mynydd Cefn-ddwy-Graig, and a 3 mile walk (**C**) in Cwm Hirnant.

START River bridge, Rhos-y-gwaliau [SH 943346] or the riverside car park, Cwm Hirnant [SH 955337] for an alternative start for Walks A and C.

DIRECTIONS See Walk 8

*R*hos-y-Gwaliau *has both a chapel and church. During the 19thC Lady Price of Rhiwlas Hall had churches built at Sarnau, Fron Goch and here to try to encourage tenants back into the Church of England. Llywarch Hen – a 6thC prince of the northern kingdom of Rheged, reputedly invited to Penllyn by a nobleman from Llanfor, is associated with nearby Rhiwaedog. Tradition says he was buried at Llanfor aged 150, having outlived his 24 sons. His last son was reportedly killed in a local battle with the Saxons, who pursued fugitives down the Hirnant..*

I Take the no through road signposted 'Rhos-y-gwaliau Centre' past the Outdoor Education Centre and rising to a junction, just past Cymerig. Here, turn LEFT along the access drive to Gelli Grin. (For **Walk B**, follow the lane ahead up the attractive Cymerig valley for 1¼ miles. Where the tarmaced lane ends at a gate becoming a track, turn right on a signposted path to rejoin the main route at point **5**.) Go through the farm and through a facing gate just beyond the house. Continue up the track to a gate, then follow the gated green track across open country – *with good views across the Hirnant valley* – later descending to pass through another farm. Continue down its access lane to pass a house to reach the bend of a forestry track. Go down the track, soon crossing the Hirnant river to reach the valley road. (For **Walk C** follow the road left along the scenic wooded river valley back to the start.)

2 Turn RIGHT along the road past Plas Aber-hirnant and Minafon, then take a signposted path through a gate on the right, and across a footbridge over the river. Go straight up the slope ahead, and after about 100 yards, bear half-LEFT up to the way-marked top corner of the forest ahead. Cross a forestry road above and go up the slope ahead, over another forestry road, and up past an abandoned hillside cottage to cross a stile in the fence by a wood corner. Bear LEFT alongside the wood boundary to cross another stile, then turn RIGHT up the nearby forestry road. Shortly, take a waymarked path on the left up through the trees to rejoin the forestry road. Go up the track ahead to cross a stile at the forest edge.

3 Head half- RIGHT to go through a gate. Continue ahead across open upland pasture – *enjoying panoramic views, with Arenig prominent ahead* – soon alongside the fence on your left. Cross a stile in the fence and go ahead across rougher pasture, soon on a fading green track, towards the forest, crossing a boggy area to cross a waymarked stile ahead, giving access to a wide firebreak in the forest. Go through the firebreak, and after a way-marked post, continue on a path through the conifers to reach a waymarked tree stump by a stream in a more open area. Cross another stream just ahead. Now go along a small depression alongside the remains of an old wall on your right for about 60 yards to reach an old lime kiln and a waymark post. Here turn RIGHT and follow a rough path through an open area of young forest for 200 yards to cross a stile into a field.

4 Turn LEFT down the field edge past the forest corner and on down the next field edge by the stream to pass two ruined buildings. Continue by the

straight ahead past rocky outcrops. Follow a clear path along the southern edge of the broad ridge of Mynydd Cefn-ddwy-Graig towards two telegraph poles with the fence always visible to your right. After passing close by the left telegraph pole, with the fence descending to the valley, keep ahead to pass to the left of another fence

stream down past a field entrance and down a small triangular reedy field to cross a stile in the corner. Cross a sleeper bridge over the stream just ahead, then go across a boggy field to a stile in the fence ahead. Continue towards Gelli-gron to pass through a small gate to the right of the cottage. Go through the wooden gate ahead, then bear RIGHT down the field to go through a gate by a stream. Go across the next large field towards a prominent white house on the skyline, over a green track and on to cross a footbridge. Continue ahead to cross the lane by a finger post.

5 Go over a ladder-stile ahead, then follow a path across a footbridge and gently rising through an area of newly planted trees to the white cottage – Encil y coed – *a converted 19thC chapel.* Here turn RIGHT to cross a ladder-stile to enter an area of Open Access. Go up the green track, past side paths and when it bends right towards a gate and a small lake beyond, continue

corner. Now angle away from the fence to go over the stone encrusted ground and down towards a cottage to reach a wall. Follow it LEFT down to cross a ladder-stile in the corner.

6 Go down the path, through a gate by a stone building, and on to cross a ladder-stile below a cottage, then steadily descend beside a stream. After a stile, continue down the line of the stream, which may be dry, and on down the field edge to reach a track just to the left of an old barn near a caravan site. Turn RIGHT past the barn, then follow the green track down the field to reach the road at Rhos-y-gwaliau. Turn RIGHT along the road back to the start.

19

WALK 10

CRAIG YR ALLOR & IS-AFON

DESCRIPTION A 7 mile walk (**A**) exploring the attractive hills south of Y Bala overlooking Llyn Tegid, following good paths and a bridleway. Allow about 4 hours. This route includes two described shorter walks of 3½ (**B**) and 2½ miles (**C**). All offer panoramic views of the lake and its surrounding hills and mountains. The main route rises to over 1500 feet to high upland pasture and moorland, taking in a new Open Access viewpoint and a section of forest, and is for the more experienced walker.

START Car park at eastern end of Llyn Tegid [SH 928354]

DIRECTIONS From the main street in Y Bala take the road (Tegid Street) opposite the White Lion Royal Hotel. Just beyond the last houses is a car park on the right near Llyn Tegid.

I Continue on the pavement along the end of Llyn Tegid – *enjoying the superb views down the lake towards the Arans* – to join the B4391. Follow it over the point where the river Dee emerges from the lake, then cross the old stone bridge and B4403 to an old stone building by the entrance to Bala Lake Railway. Bear LEFT along a path past Ty Penybont – *alongside which is the site of a motte and bailey castle* – and continue along the pavement past the entrance to Pen y Bont touring and camping park, then turn RIGHT along a track on a signposted bridleway. After about 100 yards, take a signposted path on the left angling up through the wood. At the bend of a track, continue on the signposted path up through the trees to cross a stile at the wood edge.

2 Go up the slope to a waymarked fence corner and continue on the path beneath the fence - enjoying good views. At the fence corner, follow it up to cross a stile at the top of the slope. Go half-RIGHT to cross a stile in the field corner. Continue along the next field edge and over a ladder-stile into Open Access land. Now go up the slope

ahead and on with a clear level path across the partly gorse-covered terrain, soon joining another path to cross a ladder-stile just before a white cottage – *a former 19thC chapel*. (For **Walk C**, just before the stile, turn sharp right to follow a faint path through the edge of gorse, later towards a telegraph pole on the skyline, to cross a ladder-stile. Go half-right up between gorse, then bear left across a small top and descend to a ladder-stile (broken) and through a gate to pass the front of Wenallt. Go down its access track, soon bearing right. Just beyond a stone barn, enter a field on the left and continue to cross a ladder-stile. Go half-LEFT to pass beneath a small crag and on to cross a stile 50 yards to the left of a bungalow. Descend through the wood to a track. Turn right and rejoin **Walk A** at point **6**.)

3 Follow a path to a nearby stony track. Turn RIGHT along the track through an area of replanted mixed woodland, soon passing a track on the left. After another few hundred yards, go up a waymarked path on the left between young trees, then follow a green track up to cross a ladder-stile at a great viewpoint. Continue with a faint green track rising across upland pasture. (For **Walk B**, after 75 yards head half-right down the hillside for about 250 yards to a ladder-stile and resume text at point **5**.) Continue up the track, then just before a gate, bear LEFT with the fence for about 100 yards to cross a ladder-stile. Continue ahead through a narrow reedy cutting and after a further 100 yards, gradually bear LEFT to follow a distinct green path up the hillside to cross a ladder-stile near a fence corner into Open Access land. Follow the good path across the tussocky terrain, later rising to follow the fence on the right up to a ladder-stile on the skyline. Here, turn LEFT alongside the fence to reach an initial viewpoint, then head to the highest point, marked by a small pile of stones – *offering panoramic views of Llyn Tegid, Y Bala, the Berwyns, the Arans, Cader Idris, and the Arenigs*. Return along the broad ridge, then head back towards the fence and cross the ladder-stile. Continue ahead across the open pasture of Craig yr Allor to cross a ladder-stile into a forest.

4 Follow the path through the conifers and, at a waymark post, keep ahead. At the next waymark post, turn RIGHT to follow a path on a long steady descent through the forest, later levelling out to reach a waymarked old gateway by cleared forest – *offering a good view across to the Arans*. Now descend, initially beside old fence posts then, at an embanked corner, bear LEFT down with the old boundary to a yellow-topped pole, by a waymarked gateway. Turn RIGHT and follow the waymarked bridleway through the part-cleared forest for ½ mile, eventually leaving it by a gate into Open Access land. The bridleway now contours across the bracken-covered slopes of Is-afon guided by waymark posts, later crossing a stream and going through a bridle gate. Just beyond, turn LEFT along a green bridleway, keeping to its level right fork, soon descending then following a fence to a ladder-stile. Continue near the fence, soon steadily descending to a stile/gate. Follow the fence down to a ladder-stile below – *offering a panoramic view of Llyn Tegid*.

5 Do not cross the stile. Instead, follow a green track near the fence down to cross a ladder-stile then descend the slope to cross a road. Follow the signposted path across the open hillside towards Y Bala, across a stream and a reedy area, after which it steadily descends, and meanders down to a stile. Follow the fence down to a stream near a cottage, from where the path bears half-RIGHT up to an old fence corner. Continue down alongside the fence, then go past the corner of Coed Graienyn and down a field past a house to a stile in the bottom corner. The path descends to a driveway which you follow up to nearby Bala Lake Hotel. Pass behind the main building, through the rear car park and continue along a track past farm buildings.

6 About 40 yards after passing a signposted path on the right **(Walk B)**, cross a stile on the left. Go along the field edge, over a ladder-stile and go half-RIGHT down to another ladder-stile and across a footbridge over the Bala Lake railway line, Continue to the road beyond to join your outward route.

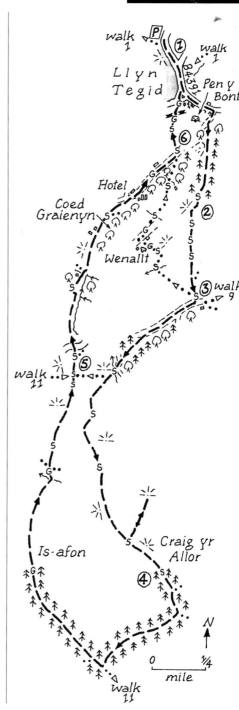

WALK 11

IS-AFON & CWM GLYN

DESCRIPTION A 6 mile walk (**A**) exploring the hills above Llangower overlooking Llyn Tegid, with great views and scenery. The route meanders across lower wooded slopes before rising steadily up Bryniau Goleu. It then follows a bridleway across the open slopes of Is-afon, reaching a height of 1246 feet/380 metres, and through a forest, before making a stunning descent into the attractive side valley of Cwm Glyn. Allow about 4 hours. The route includes an alternative 5 mile walk (**B**), taking in more of Cwm Glyn and an optional lakeside extension.

START Snowdonia National Park lakeside car park, Llangower [SH 903321]

DIRECTIONS Follow the B4403 from Y Bala along the south side of Llyn Tegid to Llangower. Go past the church to find the car park and toilets by the Bala Lake Railway halt.

The narrow gauge steam railway runs for 4½ miles between Llanuwchllyn and Y Bala along Llyn Tegid, on the track-bed of the former Great Western Ruabon – Barmouth Railway line, which closed in 1965. Rheilffordd Llyn Tegid – the first railway preservation society registered in the Welsh language – became fully operational in 1976. The hamlet of Llangower lies on the former turnpike road from Dinas Mawddwy to Y Bala/Corwen. Its small attractive church, dedicated to St. Cywair, was rebuilt in 1780-82 and restored in 1871. It is well worth a visit. It contains one of the last horse biers to be used in North Wales – reputedly until the late 19thC. 18ft in length, it was strung between horses to carry coffins. In the churchyard is an ancient yew tree.

1 Walk back along the road past the church, a telephone box and a Victorian letter-box, then turn RIGHT on to a side road. Follow it up the lower Glyn valley. Shortly, take a signposted path along a track on the left, past farm buildings and up towards a house. Follow the waymarked path behind the house and through a gate beyond. Follow the waymarked path alongside the fence through a large then small gate along the edge of mature woodland. Continue with the fence and at its corner keep ahead, soon rejoining it. About 50 yards further, the waymarked path descends alongside a stream. After about 200 yards, as the slope levels out, cross the stream. Keep ahead to cross a ladder-stile and stream, then another ladder-stile by a sheepfold. Continue alongside the fence, later passing a ladder-stile. After a stream, follow the path angling up the bracken-covered slopes of Bryniau Goleu to eventually cross a ladder-stile – *with a panoramic view along Llyn Tegid.*

2 Turn RIGHT up alongside the fence to cross a stile by a gate. Continue near the fence to follow a delightful bridleway up to a ladder-stile and across the bracken covered hillside to go through a bridle gate and across a stream. The bridleway now contours across the bracken-covered western slopes of Is-afon guided by white-topped posts to eventually enter the forest ahead by a gate. Follow the bridleway through the part cleared forest. After about ½ mile you reach a bridleway/path waymark post. (For **Walk B**, turn right to descend through the trees to a forestry road visible below. Turn right, and after 20 yards follow a waymarked path on the left down through the trees to a road. Follow it down Cwm Glyn to rejoin the main route at point **4**.) For the main walk continue ahead.

3 At an old waymarked gateway, the bridleway continues through the forest. It then crosses a stream and passes a ruined cottage, before descending a forestry track to meet another. Follow the signposted bridleway LEFT along the track for about 200 yards. After crossing the Afon Glyn – *note the small stone bridge down to your left* – at a junction of forestry tracks, go half-RIGHT up the second track. At a building, bear RIGHT to pass a cottage and outbuildings. At a small pond just beyond, bear LEFT and follow the bridleway along the forest edge, initially near a wall, up to cross a stream. At a waymarked path/bridleway junction, turn RIGHT and follow the clear path through the forest down to a stile at its edge. Go through a gap in the fence on the right just ahead, then go down the reedy field with a line of trees to your left. At the last tree, cross a stream and go ahead through reeds and on to follow another line of trees. Just beyond a water storage tank go down a sunken tree-lined path. At its end just before Cae'r-hafotty, descend

walk 10 and a ladder-stile. At the top of the slope turn RIGHT through a gateway to follow a path along the top of the stream to reach a road. Follow it down into Llangower and back to the start. A stroll along the shoreline of the lake makes a fitting finale to the walk.

Bryniau Goleu

sheepfold

Llyn Tegid

Llangower

Is-afon

N

0   ¼

mile

walk 12

walk 12

Cae'r Hafotty

Afon Glyn

ruin

walk 10

RIGHT, then at an outbuilding turn LEFT to pass further outbuildings. Continue along its delightful high-level access track – *enjoying stunning views* – later meandering down the hillside and passing a ruin to reach two cottages. Just before the gated entrance, bear RIGHT and follow the waymarked path down the old track alongside the deep wooded valley to a ladder-stile by a converted 19thC chapel. Go along the road ahead.

4 Just after joining another minor road, cross a footbridge over the river down to the left. Follow the path to the nearby concrete bridge and go up the stony track. On the bend, keep ahead to follow a path up to a ladder-stile. Follow the path over three further ladder-stiles to reach a farm, then go through a small gate on the left and up past the end of a barn. Continue up the slope past the farmhouse to cross a ladder-stile on the skyline ahead at a prominent viewpoint. Continue ahead along the old field boundary, soon descending to cross a footbridge

The church at Llangower

23

WALK 12
CWM CYNLLWYD

DESCRIPTION An exhilarating 6 mile walk (**A**) exploring both sides of attractive Cwm Cynllwyd, with excellent views. The route initially follows the Aran ridge path across Garth Fawr before heading south east along the valley, passing old farmsteads to reach the remote farming community of Talardd. It then climbs steeply reaching over 1200 feet, with stunning views of the Aran ridge, before descending a wild upland valley to ford a river, then rejoins the road. Much of the route is now waymarked. An alternative easier return from Talardd, best taken when river levels are high, is to follow the road back down the valley. Allow about 4 hours. The route includes a shorter 3 mile walk (**B**).

START Pont y Pandy by Snowdonia National Park car park, Llanuwchllyn [SH 880298]

DIRECTIONS From the A494 take the B4403 into Llanuwchllyn and go to the far end of the village to find the small car park just before the bridge over the river.

I Cross the ladder-stile by the bridge and follow a steadily rising access lane. After ⅓ mile cross a ladder-stile on the right and follow the signposted bridleway up to cross a ladder-stile. Continue up past a ladder-stile to cross another ahead to enter Open Access land. The bridleway continues to rise. At a waymark post, take the left fork (the Aran ridge path) up the hillside. After a ladder-stile, keep alongside the fence. Just before the path begins to descend, divert to the nearby cairned top of Garth Fawr for extensive views. Return to the main path and follow it down and on to reach a ladder-stile in the fence. Here turn LEFT and follow a path across rough pasture to cross a stile. The path continues up the slope ahead, later waymarked, to enter a wood. Go through the trees to cross a stile and on into a field. Go half-LEFT down to cross a stile in the fence on the left just beyond a reedy area. Continue down the next field to cross a stile near a large barn at Plas Morgan. *The mansion, now demolished, was once occupied by Peter Price – the son of a buccaneer on the Spanish Main.* Follow the track LEFT past the end of the barn. (For **Walk B** simply follow the track/lane back to the start.)

2 At a waymark post, turn sharp RIGHT down the field edge to cross a stream, then a stile by a gate. Turn RIGHT up the field to cross a stile. Turn LEFT briefly along the green track, then go across the middle of the field to cross a stile into a small wooded dingle. The path now crosses three streams by different types of footbridge, then a stile, before crossing rough wettish ground to a waymark post on the skyline. It continues across the reedy terrain, over a footbridge and on to a stile. After another footbridge and a small gate, continue towards buildings ahead to cross a stile by a gate. Go past the front of the old farmhouse, through a gate and pass to the right of a stone barn, rising to cross a ladder-stile. Continue up with the fence past another ladder-stile, then at the boundary corner bear LEFT alongside the boundary.

3 At the waymarked fence corner, continue across the field to a stile by a large boulder. Go across the next field to cross a ladder-stile by a gate. Walk alongside the fence to cross a stile in it and descend to a ladder-stile by outbuildings. Continue down a stony track to pass the front of Tyn-y-Cae. Just before the garage, turn LEFT down field edge and go through a gate in the bottom corner to reach the nearby road in the attractive side valley of Cwm Croes. Turn LEFT along the road towards Talardd, crossing the confluence of the rivers Groes and Twrch, then passing a chapel to reach a road junction. *This tiny community, situated at the junction of ancient routes, once boasted two chapels.*

4 Turn RIGHT, and at the telephone box, take the signposted path angling up to a gate. The path passes behind a house and rises across the bracken covered slope to go through a waymarked gap in the tree boundary. Now climb steeply up alongside the hawthorn boundary to reach a green track. From the nearby waymark post go half-LEFT up the bracken covered slope to a stile and continue angling up the hillside to cross a

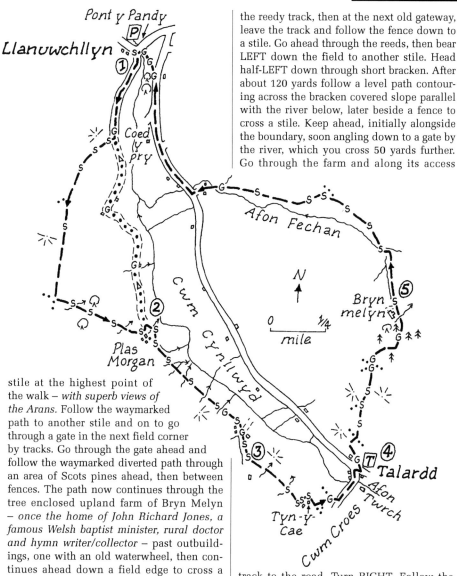

Pont y Pandy

Llanuwchllyn

Coed
y
pry

Afon Fechan

N

Cwm Cynllwyd

Plas Morgan

Bryn melyn ⑤

0   ¼
mile

Talardd ④

Afon Twrch

Tyn-y-Cae

Cwm Croes

the reedy track, then at the next old gateway, leave the track and follow the fence down to a stile. Go ahead through the reeds, then bear LEFT down the field to another stile. Head half-LEFT down through short bracken. After about 120 yards follow a level path contouring across the bracken covered slope parallel with the river below, later beside a fence to cross a stile. Keep ahead, initially alongside the boundary, soon angling down to a gate by the river, which you cross 50 yards further. Go through the farm and along its access

stile at the highest point of the walk – *with superb views of the Arans.* Follow the waymarked path to another stile and on to go through a gate in the next field corner by tracks. Go through the gate ahead and follow the waymarked diverted path through an area of Scots pines ahead, then between fences. The path now continues through the tree enclosed upland farm of Bryn Melyn – *once the home of John Richard Jones, a famous Welsh baptist minister, rural doctor and hymn writer/collector* – past outbuildings, one with an old waterwheel, then continues ahead down a field edge to cross a ladder-stile.

5 Follow the waymarked path alongside a reedy stream, gradually descending to reach the Afon Fechan in the wild upland valley. Bear LEFT to cross a ladder-stile and the river by stepping stones, then join a rising green track ahead, which soon levels out. After a second stile by a gate, continue along

track to the road. Turn RIGHT. Follow the road for just over ½ mile – *passing above Coed-y-pry where Sir Owen Morgan Edwards, who became Chief Education Inspector in 1907, was born and spent his early life.* Just past a cottage, take a signposted path through a small gate on the left. Descend steps and follow a path angling down above a wooded valley through kissing gates to reach Pont-y-Pandy.

WALK 13

BENEATH CREIGIAU LLWYN-GWERN

DESCRIPTION A 6 mile walk (**A**) exploring a little-known area of varied countryside south-west of Llanuwchllyn. The route visits beautiful river valleys, passes through forest, skirts impressive rocky hills and provides good views. Allow about 4 hours. The route includes an alternative 3½ mile walk (**B**).

START Chapel near Pont Rhyd-sarn on A494. [SH 859288]

DIRECTIONS From Llanuwchllyn follow the A494 towards Dolgellau. After about 1½ miles is a lay-by on the left just before a chapel on the right.

I Take the lane signposted to Hendre Mawr Caravan Park. Go past the site entrance and up to take a signposted path on the bend by the entrance to Hendre Fach. (For **Walk B**, follow the lane to the entrance to Maes Gwyn. Go through the gate, then head half-left up the field to go through a gate by a stream. Walk along the edge of two fields, pass by a cottage, down its access track, then follow another track right to a farm. Pass between the house and outbuilding to join the main walk at point **4**.) Go up the track, through a gate, then turn RIGHT along the field edge to go through a gate in the corner. Go through the right of two adjoining gates ahead. Keep ahead, through a gateway, then follow an old boundary down to a gate onto a lane. Follow it LEFT up to its end at Eithin Fynydd.

2 Go through the gate ahead, over a stream, then bear RIGHT to pass behind the cottage. After about 80 yards, turn LEFT alongside an old reedy boundary to cross a stile into the forest. Follow the waymarked path through the conifers, over a forestry road and on through the trees. At a signposted path junction, bear RIGHT down past a ruin to cross a footbridge and stile into a field. Turn RIGHT to cross a stile in the next

corner. Keep ahead – *views of Llyn Tegid* – later descending to go through a gate by outbuildings beneath a house and continue along its access track. At the gate entrance to Wernddu, leave the track, go past the garden corner and head across open pasture, then along the edge of a small plantation to a lane. Follow it down to a junction, then follow the road LEFT along the lower Lliw valley.

3 At a crossroad by cottages, turn LEFT up the No Through Road, then go through a gate on a signposted path. Go along a track. Shortly, cross a ladder-stile on the left, go past an old stone barn, and through a boundary gap. Turn RIGHT up to cross a stile. Go up the field, then pass round the right-hand side of outbuildings and a cottage. Just beyond the cottage, go half-LEFT up to join a gated track, which rises alongside a small wooded valley. Just beyond a barn, at a cross-road of tracks, bear RIGHT over the stream and continue up to two cottages beneath crags. From their rear, bear LEFT and walk near the fence to cross a stile to the left of the fence corner. Go half-LEFT down the reedy terrain to a green track. Follow it RIGHT to cross a footbridge and stile into the forest. Move two yards to the right, then follow the path through the dense forest guided by yellow spots or tapes on trees. After two streams, the path rises with a wall to your left, before passing its corner by another stream. Keep ahead to leave the forest by a stile. Go ahead down the field towards the Arans and through a wall gap in the bottom right corner. Continue through the bracken just above the stream/boundary, gently descending to join a green track. Follow it down to go through a gate by a farm. Cross the stream and turn RIGHT down behind the house.

4 At outbuildings bear RIGHT to recross the stream and go through a gate. Follow the lower of two green tracks, soon overlooking an area of cleared forest. After a gate, the track continues beneath Creigiau Llwyn-gwern. After another gate at the former forest corner, continue briefly on the track, then follow the boundary on your right up the slope to a stile in the corner. Continue ahead to join a rising faint green track. After a ladder-stile follow the fence through two fields beneath Moel Caws. After a gate, the path angles away from the fence corner through a long field towards Coed Penaran to go through a gate just above the infant Afon Dyfrdwy/River Dee.

5 Turn LEFT alongside the fence. Soon, follow an old reedy track contouring around rough pasture to go through a gateway. *Nearby is the site of the old settlement of Tre Eurych (meaning 'worker in gold') containing remains of enclosures, platform houses and a possible millwheel pit.* Continue down a green track to a forestry road. Take the waymarked path opposite down to a gate and cross the river by stepping stones. Go through a gate by the house at Garneddwen Halt – *a passing section on the former Ruabon-Barmouth railway line.* Cross the forestry road and go up a green track opposite to cross the A494. Turn LEFT, then go up a forestry road on the right.

6 Just before a gate, turn LEFT through reeds to cross a stile 25 yards away. Continue across the reedy field to reach the entrance to Tyn y Cefn. Just beyond at a finger post, go half-RIGHT along the field edge, through a gate, across another field, and over a stile. Keep ahead between boundaries to cross a stile into an area of cleared forest. Cross a footbridge, then go half-LEFT across the rough ground, past a waymark post to follow a clearer path to a stile. leaving the forest. *In a nearby field is the site of a Roman Practice Camp, and on higher slopes is a Roman watchstone.*

Just beyond turn RIGHT, cross a stream, and follow an old reedy track to descend to a ladder-stile onto a track. Follow it LEFT, past caravans, over the river, and go along the lane ahead to the A494.

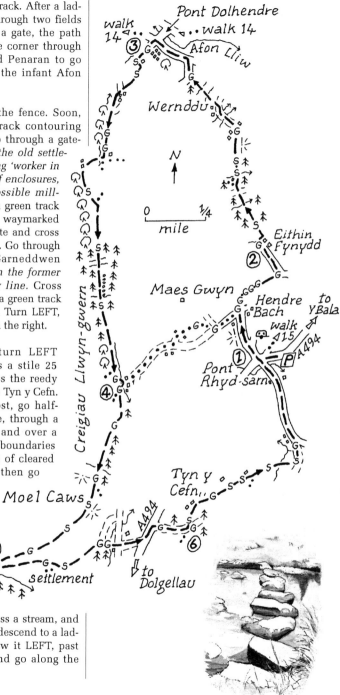

27

WALK 14
CASTELL CARNDOCHAN & CWM LLIW

DESCRIPTION A 5½ mile walk exploring both sides of the lower Lliw valley, with extensive views and featuring an early climb (optional) to an impressive remote ancient hilltop castle (1115 feet/340 metres), now accessible in Open Access land. Afterwards the route follows a bridleway into attractive open upland country, then down to cross the river. After passing through Coed Wenallt, the route rises up the other side of the valley to follow a scenic high-level road, before returning mostly by field paths. Allow about 3½ hours. The route can be undertaken as two shorter walks of 3 miles and 2¾ miles by utilising the linking section of road from and to point 3.

START Pont Dolhendre [SH 853308]

DIRECTIONS From Y Bala follow the A494 past Llyn Tegid, then just before Llanuwchllyn, turn right on a minor road signposted to Trawsfynydd. Follow the road for about 1½ miles to reach a telephone box by a bridge over the river (Pont Dolhendre), where there is limited roadside parking.

*C*astell Carndochan – *a ridgetop castle probably built by Llywelyn ap Iorwerth in the early 13thC to defend the easy road of attack up Pennant-lliw. It contained a round tower at its northern end, a D-shaped one to the south, and a square building in the centre. In those days Penllyn belonged to Powys. Llywelyn later annexed Penllyn and it became part of Gwynedd. For a few generations, the noblemen of Penllyn still chose to be buried in Powys. Near the castle was a gold mine, once owned by John Bright, a Quaker M.P, which was worked between 1860-1910.*

I Cross the bridge over the Afon Lliw and walk up the road. At cross-roads, turn RIGHT and follow the lane up past cottages, then continue with a stony track beneath Castell Carndochan. Just before the track bends over a stream, go through the first gate up to your left. Follow an old reedy green track initially alongside a wall, soon bending away and rising across the hillside. After levelling out, the track bends sharp left up the slope then disappears in reeds. Briefly continue in the same direction towards the craggy top of Castell Carndochan then angle up onto the high ground to your right containing a large rock. Continue to the distinctive rocky hilltop castle for great all-round views – *including Llyn Tegid, the Berwyns, the Arans and Arenig Fawr.* Retrace your steps down from the castle, then just below in a small depression full of stones take a clear path on the right descending northwest. It soon angles down across the initially boulder-covered slope. After it levels out, descend to the end of a fence below to rejoin the outward track back down to the gate.

2 Follow the stony track across the stream (note the old stone clapper bridge) and up through the forest, then open upland pasture – *with Moel Llyfnant and Arenig Fawr prominent ahead* – to eventually reach a house. Pass round the right-hand corner of the attached stone outbuilding. Go through the first gate on your right opposite outbuildings. Cross the field and go through a gate ahead, then go half-RIGHT to go through a low wall just to the right of a tree. Go down the field and through a gate in the bottom right-hand wall corner. Follow the boundary on your left to go through a gate ahead, then descend the steep slope to cross the large footbridge over the Afon Lliw below. Go through trees to a forestry track. Follow it RIGHT through Coed Wenallt, soon bending away from the river to an open aspect. At its end, where the track levels out, take a path angling down on the right. Follow it through the trees down to a gate, then go through a caravan park to a road. Continue along the road.

3 Opposite the caravan park entrance go through a set of wooden gates. Go half-RIGHT to a gate. Continue in the same direction across the next field to cross a stream and on through a gate beyond. About 50 yards further go through a gate up on your left. Walk towards a telegraph post ahead. Here turn RIGHT up an old boundary and

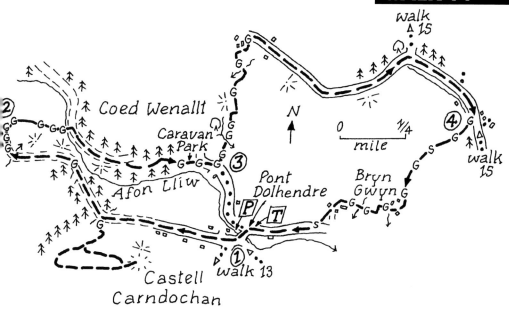

after about 100 yards turn LEFT through a gap, then go up the next field to go through a gate in the corner. Now follow a rising green track, soon bending LEFT over a stream and through a gate. The track now disappears, but continue ahead for about 100 yards, then go half-RIGHT up towards a farm ahead. Follow the track round its outbuildings, then turn sharp RIGHT along its access track, and on past a house. Continue along the road – *enjoying panoramic views.* Later it begins a steady descent.

4 Just before a gate across the road by a house go half-RIGHT on a signposted path to pass through a gate. Go across the field and through a gate in the corner. Continue alongside the tree boundary on your right to cross a stile in the corner. Now head half-LEFT to go through a gate in the corner. Walk down the field edge, then bear half-LEFT to pass through a gate near a farm. Continue down a track, then bear RIGHT through the farmyard. Pass the front of Bryn Gwyn and through a gate at the end of a small wood. Follow a track round for about 100 yards to a gate in the field corner. Here turn RIGHT along the field edge on a way-marked permissive path to go through a gate in the other corner. Continue ahead, through another gate and pass to the right of farm buildings, soon bending LEFT down a rough track. At more outbuildings, leave the bend of the track to go straight down the field to cross a stile onto a road. Turn RIGHT and follow the road back to the start.

Castell Carndochan

29

WALK 15
Y LORDSHIP

DESCRIPTION A 6 mile walk exploring the undulating landscape south and west of Parc. The route uses field paths, forest tracks and quiet lanes, passing places of historical interest, and provides good views. Allow about 3½ hours.

START Parc [SH 877339]

DIRECTIONS Take the A494 out of Y Bala towards Dolgellau, and after about 3½ miles, just past Glanllyn Caravan and Camping Park, turn right to follow the road signposted to Parc. Descend into the village, passing the school, and over a bridge to park tidily on the roadside.

*P*arc *is a small community named after the area's historical association as a hunting park, where the Burgesses of Y Bala exercised their rights to hunt, given to them at the establishment of the town. Parc is also known as the birthplace of Merched y Wawr – the Welsh Women's Institute – established here in 1967, and the area is important for Welsh penillion singing (penillion means 'verses' in Welsh).*

I Cross the bridge over the river and take the first turning on the left by Hen Bost opposite the school. Follow the access track to a farm and cross a stile just beyond the house. Keep ahead, and at the fence corner go half-LEFT across the field, over a stream and on to cross another by a waymarked fence corner. Continue alongside the fence to cross a sleeper bridge and a stile. Go up to the fence corner and across the middle of the field to go through a gap in the boundary ahead. Keep ahead on a path across the next field, and after crossing a stream, continue ahead, soon alongside a fence above outbuildings at Plas Madog – *an old manor house*. At a fence corner, negotiate a boggy area, then angle away from the fence up to a stile by a finger post onto a road. Go through the gate opposite and on across the field to go through a waymarked gate ahead. Continue across the next field to cross a stile/sleeper bridge. Turn LEFT. At the fence corner keep ahead – *with good views of Llyn Tegid* – to cross a stile in the corner. Cross a stream, then head half-RIGHT across a large field to go through a waymarked gateway near the corner and on to reach a track by a finger post.

2 Bear RIGHT with the track past sheep-folds and up through a waymarked gate. Continue along the track and through another gate. On the bend, keep ahead on the sign-posted path along the reed and gorse covered edge of a cleared forest, near the fence – *with good views ahead of the Arans and Cader Idris* – to cross a sleeper bridge then a stile at its end into a field. Continue ahead across the large field to go through a gate in the far left-hand corner. Follow the signposted path with the fence on your right to cross a stile in the corner. Keep ahead along the bottom of the slope – *up to your left is the site of Caer Gai Roman fort* – soon descending to cross a stile by the stream/plantation.

3 Continue down the edge of reedy terrain to cross a stile and footbridge on the right. Now follow a track LEFT to go through a gate onto a lane by Erw Fron. Turn RIGHT along a track, soon passing the unassuming stone house of Weirglodd Wen. *This was once the home of Michael Jones, who was minister at the nonconformist chapel you will pass shortly. After a quarrel with part of the congregation, he moved out of the chapel house to Weirglodd Wen, where he founded a nonconformist academy. He then established it in Y Bala as an Independent College and served as its Principal. His son, Michael D. Jones, (1822-98), who also lived in Weirglodd Wen, succeeded his father as Principal. He was a staunch Liberal and Welsh nationalist, and one of the people behind a plan to found a 'New Wales' in Patagonia, South America. In 1865, 153 men, women and children sailed from Liverpool to Patagonia where they established a Welsh community amongst the Indians – establishing townships, building chapels and holding their own eisteddfodau. Patagonia became part of Argentina, and Spanish gradually replaced the Welsh language. Their descendants still maintain strong ties with Wales and many still speak Welsh.* Go through a gate beyond the house, then bear LEFT past a stone barn,

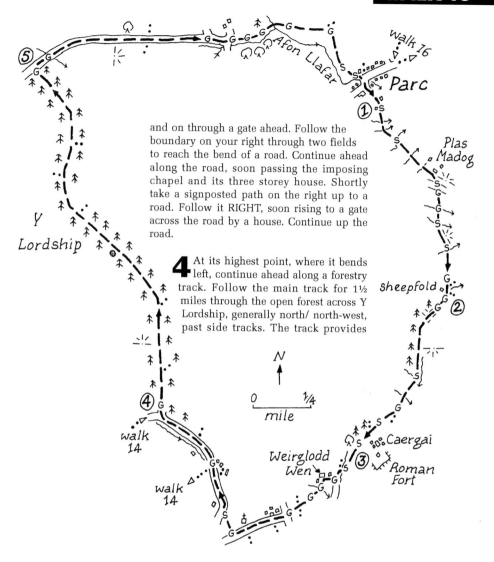

and on through a gate ahead. Follow the boundary on your right through two fields to reach the bend of a road. Continue ahead along the road, soon passing the imposing chapel and its three storey house. Shortly take a signposted path on the right up to a road. Follow it RIGHT, soon rising to a gate across the road by a house. Continue up the road.

4 At its highest point, where it bends left, continue ahead along a forestry track. Follow the main track for 1½ miles through the open forest across Y Lordship, generally north/ north-west, past side tracks. The track provides

easy walking and good views of Arenig Fawr ahead. After passing a small pool and old quarry on the left, keep ahead at the next junction. It later becomes a narrow reedy green track which eventually reaches a lane.

5 Follow it RIGHT – *enjoying good open views towards the Berwyns* – later descending to reach a road junction. Continue ahead, and after about 200 yards, take a signposted path along the access track to Fferm

Ty-Du. After 50 yards, go through a way-marked gate on the right and follow a gated track alongside the stream. At the end of the track, cross a footbridge over the Afon Llafar. Now go half-RIGHT, through a gate, and on across the next long field to a gate in the far narrow corner. Go across the middle of the next field to cross a ladder-stile near the river. Go across the field to cross a footbridge and stile in the far corner and continue to the road by the bridge at Parc.

MOEL Y GARNEDD

DESCRIPTION A 7¾ mile (**A**) or 3½ mile (**B**) walk exploring the upland area west of Y Bala, featuring Moel y Garnedd (1180 feet)/360 metres), now a designated Open Access area, and extensive views. The route rises in stages with a bridleway up to moorland, which it crosses to reach the summit of Moel y Garnedd. The main walk then descends and continues for ½ mile across open moorland before following field paths to Parc. It returns by a quiet country road, then moorland, field and woodland paths. Allow about 5 hours. The route is for experienced walkers who enjoy wild open places, requires careful navigation across moorland, and should be avoided in poor visibility. The route includes two less demanding shorter walks of 2¾ (**C**) and 1½ (**D**) miles.

START Fronfeuno Snowdonia National Park lakeside car park [SH 917351] or car park opposite Llanycil church [SH 914349].

DIRECTIONS Leave Y Bala on the A494 towards Dolgellau. Fronfeuno is the second car park on the left 400 yards after the entrance to Llyn Tegid..

I From Fronfeuno car park walk west along the pavement towards Llanycil. Just after the Llanycil sign, cross the road and go through Fron Feuno farm entrance. Follow the signposted bridleway up the track. After about 120 yards, go half-RIGHT up the waymarked bridleway and through a small gate. The bridleway rises through trees to another small gate, then passes through a waymarked larger gate and continues up a track past cottages. The track rises more steeply before levelling out. As it starts to rise again, at a waymark post, go half-LEFT on a path, soon by the boundary, to go through a gate. Go across the field, through a waymarked gate and along the hedge-lined track to pass through a gate by a barn. (For **Walk D**, go through the adjoining gate, and follow a waymarked path through two fields to join the returning main route at a finger post.)

2 Go through the farm and along its access lane. On the bend, go through a waymarked gate ahead into Open Access land. Follow the reedy path to a waymark post. Here head half-LEFT over springy moorland, then aim for the left-hand side of the first clump of five trees on the mid-slope ahead, about 150 yards to the left of a wall/fence. Just beyond the trees is a cross-path. (For **Walk C**, follow it left, descending past a rock outcrop and on to cross a ladder-stile. Continue to a gate in the right-hand field corner and go through the caravan park. Turn left off the driveway to pass between two cottages to resume text at point **7**.) Continue up to a second group of trees.

3 A few yards beyond, in line with a ladder-stile in the boundary to the right, bear LEFT down the slope to follow a clear path rising steadily across open moorland, passing a small tree then a fence/wall corner. Continue up the path – *Arenig appears ahead* – keeping to the left fork to pass beneath a small rocky escarpment. *From its top, are good views of the Llantisilio Mountains, the Berwyns, Llyn Tegid, the Arans, Cader Idris, and the Arenigs.* Where the path clips the crag above gorse, before it bends and descends, head towards the high ground to your right to follow a path up the tussocky slope and across the broad top of Moel y Garnedd to a trig point. (For **Walk B**, work your way down the south eastern slopes towards a cottage almost hidden by trees to cross a ladder-stile at their right-hand end at point **6**.) Just beyond the trig point, head slightly right down its western slope, passing between areas of reeds to join a clear path running down its lower slope. From the bottom of the slope the path heads towards the distant summit of Arenig Fawr.

4 After about 100 yards, the path reaches rougher reedy moorland and bears half-left. Here, leave the path and continue straight ahead towards the summit of Arenig Fawr on intermittent paths. Keep on this line, later descending to cross more tussocky reedy terrain, then a stream to cross a stile in the fence by an old gate, marked by a tall yellow-topped pole. Cross a stream, then

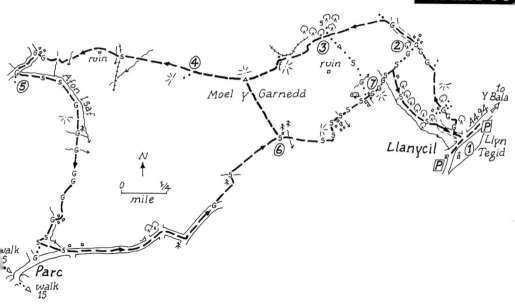

go on to join an old embanked boundary ahead, which you follow past a nearby ruin and down to its end. Go ahead across the bracken-covered field, soon descending. Just before the fence, bear LEFT to follow a path down to a track. Cross the nearby stream and follow the track up to pass a ruined farm to reach a road. Follow it LEFT. After crossing the Afon Isaf, take a signposted path through a gate on the left.

5 Go ahead along the edge of three fields (stiles) above the river. After a gate, continue through two fields towards the Arans, then alongside the next field boundary to pass through two gates. Follow a green track down to a farm. At the gable end of the house, keep straight ahead to pass between outbuildings, then go half-RIGHT to cross an old gate and a stream. Turn LEFT down the field edge, over a stile, and follow the boundary on the left to cross a ladder-stile. Go half-LEFT to a stile in the corner onto a road. Follow it for about 1 mile, then take a signposted path through a kissing gate on the left. Go along the field edge, then follow the side of a small plantation round to cross a stile and footbridge into Open Access land. Now head half-RIGHT across the moorland

below Moel y Garnedd to follow an intermittent path, later passing a finger post, to cross a ladder-stile by a gate and trees.

6 Go past the cottage, over its access track and a stream, and on across the large field to a ladder-stile by a gate. Follow a track to a farm to cross a nearby ladder-stile. Follow the permissive path up to another ladder-stile/sleeper-bridge. Turn RIGHT and cross the ladder-stile ahead. Go across the field, over a stile and on across the next undulating field to a stile into a caravan park. Go ahead past a house and across the driveway to walk between two cottages.

7 Go through a gate into a field, then the small gate ahead. Descend the field to another small gate and cross a footbridge and a stile. Go through bracken and up the field to a finger post. Here, turn RIGHT and go down the edge of the long reedy field, past a rising path and a demolished stone building, to cross a stile at the bottom into a wood. Continue through the attractive woodland. After a stile, go down the slope and follow the waymarked path to an access track. Follow it down to the road and back to the start.

WALK 17
TRYWERYN TRAIL

DESCRIPTION A delightful 1½ mile way-marked riverside nature trail along the interna-tional renowned wooded white water stretch of the Trywern to the fish trap below Llyn Celyn reservoir. A more detailed Trail booklet is avail-able from the Centre, which has a cafe. Allow about an hour. Note that the river level can rise rapidly when water is released from the dam above, so heed the warning signs.
START Canolfan Trywern – The National Whitewater Centre [SH 892401]
DIRECTIONS Canolfan Trywern lies just off the A4212 Y Bala-Trawsfynydd road, about 4 miles from Y Bala. Use the main car park beyond the Centre.

In the 1960s there occurred a sad chap-ter in modern Welsh history, when the Welsh speaking community of Capel Celyn, with its cottages, farms, school, chapel and churchyard, despite national protests, was drowned by Liverpool City Corporation to create the reservoir of Llyn Celyn. One of the unexpected consequences of controlled releases of water into the Afon Trywern down to the Dee, has been the development of the river for kayaking and canoeing since the mid 1970s. It has has pioneered whitewater rafting in the UK. and hosted international competitions and world championships.

From the centre of the car park, take the signposted Trywern Trail under the for-mer railway line, then bear RIGHT to cross a footbridge. Follow the path through a small island to cross another footbridge. Continue on the waymarked riverside Trail to reach the Celyn Fish Trap, where you bear RIGHT along an access road. At a junction turn RIGHT, then go through a gate on the right by waymark 16 and follow the track through the trees to another gate. Briefly rejoin your out-ward route, then continue on a higher stony track to pass between buildings to reach the main car park. From its entrance follow the riverside path to cross the bridge over the river. Now continue with the riverside trail, near the former Bala-Ffestiniog railway line. *Opened in 1882, and extended to Blaenau in 1883, it carried passengers and freight, especially slate from the nearby Arenig quar-ries, until its closure in 1961. The bend in the river by the Centre opposite is known as 'The Elbow' from its shape and what you bang when things go wrong!* Cross the footbridge over the river, then follow the trail to the centre and back to the car park.

WALK 18
CRAIG Y GARN

DESCRIPTION A 3¾ mile walk (**A**) featur-ing a short section of the Tryweryn Trail, the attractive upland area to the north of Canolfan Trywern, including the craggy top of Craig y Garn (1512 feet/461 metres), now an Open Access area, offering extensive all-round views. The route follows the riverside path, then rises in stages to the base of Craig y Garn, before making a short ascent to its summit, returning to cross the fast-flowing Afon Hesgyn and fol-lowing field paths to rejoin the outward route. The ascent up Craig y Garn can be omitted, making a 3 mile walk (**B**). The walk can also be extended to incorporate the longer section of the Tryweryn Trail.
START Canolfan Trywern – as Walk 17

From the car park entrance follow the waymarked riverside path to cross the bridge over the river and continue with the riverside trail, near the former Bala-Ffestiniog railway line, passing the Centre opposite. Cross the footbridge over the river and con-tinue ahead to the A4212. Turn RIGHT along the road edge with care, soon passing a cha-pel. After a further 200 yards, cross the road and go up a gated access lane. At a cottage, bear RIGHT to go through a gate by a shed and on up the tree-lined path to cross a stile and a stream just beyond. Follow the bound-ary and stream on your left up to another stile. Continue ahead to join a green track to the right of gorse. It rises steadily near the stream. When it bends left across the stream go through a waymarked gate ahead. *Looking back Llyn Celyn can be seen.* Keep ahead along the edge of rough upland pasture, soon following a level track – with views unfolding of the Llangwm hills ahead.

2 When it disappears just beyond a large stone slab, as the ground ahead begins to descend, bear LEFT down the reed-covered slope, then go through a gap in the old wall on your left. Follow the path guided by yellow-topped poles to cross a stream, then a stile. Go up the field edge by an old wall, then 80 yards before a corner, go through a wall gap and angle up to cross a wall by the remains of an upland farm. (For **Walk B** resume text at point **3**.)

Craig y Garn

ruin

ruin

③

②

WALK 18

N

WALK 17

P Centre

0   ¼

mile

Fish Trap

Afon Tryweryn

Turn RIGHT and follow the boundary up to a stile by a gate to enter Open Access land. Just above bear RIGHT on a path which rises past a small wood. When opposite a gate at the wood corner, turn LEFT and follow a path up the slope. After levelling out the path rises half-LEFT to pass beneath crags onto the top of Craig y Garn just north of its highest point. From its summit cairn and nearby large rock with a memorial slate, are great views of Llyn Celyn, the Arenigs and the Arans. Either descend the same way or go onto the adjoining high crags, then work your way down the south-eastern slopes to the right-hand wood corner to return to the ruin.

3 Follow the level old green track leading away from the ruin, skirting the slopes of Craig y Garn – *with a good view of Llyn Celyn and the Arenigs* – then descending to pass in front of a ruined house. A path now continues to a footbridge over the Afon Hesgyn, which you cross. Bear LEFT up an old track, then follow a stream up to the small plantation above. Here turn LEFT to cross a stile and go along the field edge, past a stile, then follow the fence on the right to cross a ladder-stile and footbridge. Continue down the edge of a wood and over another ladder-stile near the corner. Turn RIGHT and follow the path down past a pylon and through a gate by a cottage. Swing sharp LEFT down to cross a stone bridge over the river, and go past cottages to follow your outward route back to Canolfan Tryweryn, taking the riverside trail to the Centre and the car park.

WALK 19
Y BALA TO LLANUWCHLLYN

DESCRIPTION A 7 mile scenic linear walk (part 1 of a Llyn Tegid circular walk) across the foothills on the north west side of Llyn Tegid, reaching a height of 918 feet/280 metres, and offering good views of Arenig and the Arans. This route was originally researched for a long distance trail following the river Dee, and it has now been adopted by the Snowdonia National Park Authority, which has installed new stiles and waymarked it to Llanuwchllyn. Allow about 4½ hours. Refreshments in Llanuwchllyn at the Eagle Inn and Bala Lake Railway Cafe in season.

START Loch Cafe/Lakeside car park entrance SH 921355

DIRECTIONS Take the Arriva X94 regular bus service from the bus stop by Station Road at the southern end of Llanuwchllyn. Use roadside parking or nearby SNP car park (See Walk 12) in Llanuwchllyn. Alight near the Leisure Centre in Y Bala and walk along the road to the start. Bus timetable from Bws Gwynedd (01286 679535), Traveline (0870 6082608) or TIC. Another option is to combine the walk with a scenic return ride on Bala Lake Railway – (01678 540666).

1 From Loch Cafe and the entrance to the lakeside car park go along the pavement above the tree-lined edge of the lake, past Fronfeuno Snowdonia National Park car park. Just beyond the Llanycil road sign cross the road and go through the Fron Feuno farm entrance gateway on a signposted bridleway. Follow the track up to a finger post on the bend. Here, go half-LEFT to follow the waymarked path up to a stile in a fence corner. Follow the path through the wood then up the right-hand edge of a long reedy field to a finger post at the top. Bear LEFT, then angle away from the boundary down to cross a stile/footbridge. After a small gate go up the field to another small gate, and across the next field. Go through a gate and on between cottages. Cross the caravan site's driveway and continue ahead past a house to a stile.

2 Go across the undulating field to a stile below the final rise. Go towards the farm to cross a ladder-stile and keep ahead along a green track to cross a sleeper bridge and ladder-stile. Go down the field edge to cross a ladder-stile near farm buildings. Go briefly ahead, then bear RIGHT up a green track to reach a ladder-stile. Head towards a distant house and a ladder-stile just beyond. Go across the moorland towards a small plantation, past a finger post – *with a good view of Arenig* – to cross a footbridge/stile at the plantation corner. Walk round the edge of the plantation and along the field edge to a road. Follow it LEFT for ⅓ mile to the signposted path and stile on the right.

3 Go along the field gradually angling away from the fence to a stile. Now follow the stiled waymarked path through several fields to a farm. Pass to the left of conifers and buildings, following a green track up to a ladder-stile. Keep ahead, soon following the boundary on your right to cross a ladder-stile near the fence corner. Go half-RIGHT to follow telegraph poles down to a ladder-stile. Descend steeply to a ladder-stile below onto a track. Follow it LEFT round past Llwynmawr-isaf, then follow its driveway, later alongside the river, to the road. Turn LEFT, then RIGHT by cottages to follow the signposted SNP path through a gate and up the

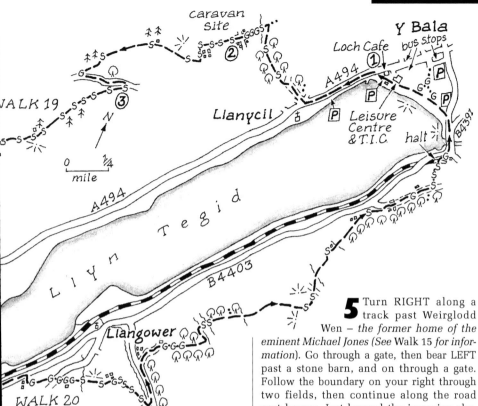

access track (Tyn Llechwedd) to a finger post, where the track splits.

4 Follow the right fork past sheepfolds up through a waymarked gate. Follow the track through another gate. On the bend, keep ahead on the signposted path along the reed and gorse covered edge of a cleared forest, near the fence – *with good views of the Arans and Cader Idris* – to cross a sleeper bridge then a stile at its end. Continue ahead across the large field to go through a gate in the far left-hand corner. Follow the signposted path by the fence to a stile. Keep ahead along the bottom of the slope soon descending to a stile by the stream/plantation. Continue down the edge of reedy terrain to cross a stile and footbridge on the right. Follow a track to a lane by Erw Fron.

5 Turn RIGHT along a track past Weirglodd Wen – *the former home of the eminent Michael Jones (See* Walk 15 *for information).* Go through a gate, then bear LEFT past a stone barn, and on through a gate. Follow the boundary on your right through two fields, then continue along the road past houses. Just beyond the imposing chapel, take the signposted path on the left and follow this chapel path to the A494. Cross the bridge with care, go past houses then cross the road and follow the pavement into Llanuwchllyn. *At the village entrance are the statues of two eminent Welshmen who were born here. Sir Owen Morgan Edwards (1858-1920), regularly punished for speaking Welsh whilst at school, later became Chief Inspector of the new Welsh Education Department established in 1907. He actively promoted Welsh learning, writing many books and magazines. His son – Sir Ifan ab Owen Edwards (1895-1970) founded the Urdd Gobaith Cymru (The Welsh League of Youth) – which blends together culture, artistic activity, outdoor pursuits and Christian piety.* Continue through the village past the Eagles inn and church to reach Station Road.

WALK 20

LLANUWCHLLYN TO Y BALA

DESCRIPTION A 7 mile linear walk (part **2** of a Llyn Tegid circuit) from Llanuwchllyn, meandering across the foothills on the south east side of Llyn Tegid, reaching a height of 1083 feet/ 330 metres and enjoying extensive views of the lake throughout. The Bala Lake Railway (four trains daily and cafe in season – tel. 01678 540666) also provides an opportunity to combine the walk with a scenic lakeside railway ride.

START Station Road, Llanuwchllyn SH 878299

DIRECTIONS Take the Arriva X94 regular bus service from Y Bala to the bus stop by Station Road at the southern end of Llanuwchllyn. Where you catch the bus is dependent on your choice of start. If using the lakeside SNP car park by Loch cafe, the bus can be taken from near Stryd-y-Fron on the A494, past the entrance to the Leisure Centre. If starting from the town centre, there is a bus stop near Ye Olde Bulls Head on High Street, and a choice of return link paths from the lake at the end.

I Go along Station Road signposted to Bala Lake Railway to reach the station, where refreshments are available when open. Go through the car park, past the engine sheds and alongside the line. (This is a permissive section by kind agreement of the Railway. Do not walk along the track.) About 100 yards beyond the last shed cross the line to go through a kissing gate and continue up the reedy field to the road. Follow it past Felindre, then cross a ladder-stile on the right. Go half-LEFT up two fields, then follow an access lane up to a farm. Go between outbuildings and past the house to go through a gate beyond. Follow the boundary on your left down to cross a stream. Bear LEFT down the long field edge to cross a stile and a stream, then follow the edge of a sunken way to a ladder-stile and a lane. Continue with care along the nearby B4403 past Pentrepiod halt and a house close by the railway.

2 Shortly, turn up the access track to Ffynongower. At the house, swing sharp LEFT up through a gate and on across the slope up to a gate and a lane. Go through the gate opposite and follow the track up to pass Cae-glas (gates), then go along the bottom field edge to cross a ladder-stile/ footbridge in a narrow dingle. Follow an old field boundary to a ladder-stile. Go down towards a farm to pass to the right of outbuildings. After a small gate, cross the nearby ladderstile, then follow the path over three further ladder-stiles to reach a stony track. Follow it down and just before a bridge over the river, follow a path to cross a footbridge just upstream. Bear LEFT and go up to a road. Follow it along the valley.

3 Take a signposted path along a track on the right, past farm buildings and up towards a house. Follow the path behind the house and through a gate beyond. Follow the waymarked path alongside the fence through a large then small gate. At the fence corner, keep ahead, soon rejoining it. After a further 50 yards, the waymarked path descends alongside a stream. After about 200 yards, as the slope levels out, cross the stream. Keep ahead to cross a ladder-stile and a stream, then another ladder-stile by a sheepfold. Continue alongside the fence, later passing a ladder-stile. After a stream, follow the

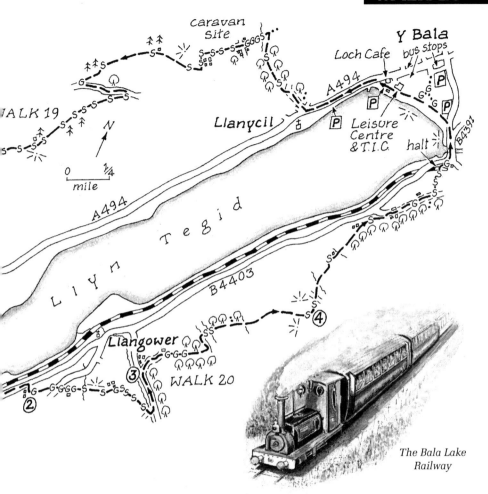

The Bala Lake Railway

path angling up the bracken-covered hillside to eventually cross a ladder-stile at a great viewpoint.

4 Join a track just beyond and follow it down to cross a ladder-stile, then descend the slope to cross a road. Follow the signposted path across the open hillside towards Y Bala. After crossing a stream and a reedy area, it steadily descends, soon meandering down to a stile. Follow the fence on your left down to a stream near a cottage, then follow the path up to an old fence corner. Continue down alongside the fence, then go past a wood corner and down a field past a house to a stile in the corner. The path descends to a driveway which you follow up to nearby Bala Lake Hotel. Pass behind the main building, through the rear car park and continue along a track past farm buildings. About 40 yards after passing a signposted path on the right, cross a stile on the left, and go down two fields, then across a footbridge over Bala Lake Railway and on to the B4403. Cross the old bridge opposite, go along the B4391 and follow the pavement along the end of the lake. At a car park, take a tarmac path near the shoreline of the lake, past two side paths leading to a car park and town centre, to eventually pass behind the Leisure Centre to reach the lakeside SNP car park.

PRONUNCIATION

These basic points should help non-Welsh speakers

Welsh	English equivalent
c	always hard, as in cat
ch	as in the Scottish word loch
dd	as th in then
f	as f in of
ff	as ff in off
g	always hard as in got
ll	no real equivalent. It is like 'th' in then, but with an 'L' sound added to it, giving 'thlan' for the pronunciation of the Welsh 'Llan'.

In Welsh the accent usually falls on the last-but-one syllable of a word.

KEY TO THE MAPS

- ➡ Walk route and direction
- ═ Metalled road
- ─ ─ ─ Unsurfaced road
- • • • • Footpath/route adjoining walk route
- ~~~ River/stream
- 🌲 Trees
- ▬▬ Railway
- **G** Gate
- **S** Stile
- **F.B.** Footbridge
- ☀ Viewpoint
- P Parking
- T Telephone
- 🚐 Caravan site

THE COUNTRY CODE

- Be safe – plan ahead and follow any signs
- Leave gates and property as you find them
- Protect plants and animals, and take your litter home
- Keep dogs under close control
- Consider other people

Some routes cross land where walkers have a legal right of access under the CRoW Act 2000, introduced in May 2005. Open Access land is detailed on OS Explorer maps OL18, OL 23 and 255 which cover this area. This access can be subject to restrictions and closure for land management or safety reasons for up to 28 days a year. Please respect any notices. The Countryside Council for Wales website (www.ccw.gov.uk) provides updated information on any closures.

I wish to thank Gwynedd Council for continuing to maintain footpaths in this area. Special thanks are also due to Ifor Owen of Llanuwchllyn for sharing his wonderful knowledge of this area's history.

David Berry

Published by
Kittiwake
3 Glantwymyn Village Workshops, Glantwymyn, Machynlleth, Montgomeryshire SY20 8LY

© Text & map research: David Berry 2008
© Maps & illustrations: Kittiwake 2008.

First edition 2004. Part revision 2004. Reprints 2005, 2006, 2007. New edition 2008

Illustrations by Morag Perrott
Cover photographs: David Berry – large: Llyn Tegid, inset: Llangower church
Care has been taken to be accurate. However neither the author nor the publisher can accept responsibility for any errors which may appear, or their consequences. If you are in doubt about any access, check before you proceed.
Printed by MWL, Pontypool.
ISBN: 978 1 902302 54 6